TEACH US TO PRAY

PRACTICAL WRESTLING AND A CHRIST-GIVEN MODEL TO ENHANCE OUR PRAYER LIVES

Travis Blake

WESTBOW
PRESS®
A DIVISION OF THOMAS NELSON
& ZONDERVAN

This book is a work of non-fiction. Unless otherwise noted, the author
and the publisher make no explicit guarantees as to the accuracy of
the information contained in this book and in some cases, names of
people and places have been altered to protect their privacy.

WestBow Press books may be ordered through booksellers or by contacting:

WestBow Press
A Division of Thomas Nelson & Zondervan
1663 Liberty Drive
Bloomington, IN 47403
www.westbowpress.com
844-714-3454

Because of the dynamic nature of the Internet, any web addresses or
links contained in this book may have changed since publication and may
no longer be valid. The views expressed in this work are solely those
of the author and do not necessarily reflect the views of the publisher,
and the publisher hereby disclaims any responsibility for them.

Any people depicted in stock imagery provided by Getty Images are
models, and such images are being used for illustrative purposes only.
Certain stock imagery © Getty Images.

Scripture quotations are taken from the Holy Bible, New Living Translation,
Copyright © 1996, 2004, 2015 by Tyndale House Foundation. Used by permission
of Tyndale House Publishers, Inc., Carol Stream, Illinois 60188. All rights reserved.

World's Last Night by CS Lewis © copyright 1960 CS Lewis Pte Ltd.
Reflection on the Psalms by CS Lewis © copyright 1958 CS Lewis Pte Ltd.
Extracts reprinted with permission.

ISBN: 978-1-9736-9925-5 (sc)
ISBN: 978-1-9736-9926-2 (hc)
ISBN: 978-1-9736-9924-8 (e)

Library of Congress Control Number: 2023909743

Print information available on the last page.

WestBow Press rev. date: 05/30/2023

CONTENTS

PART 2 - A CHRIST-GIVEN MODEL

ACKNOWLEDGMENTS

A special thanks to Lori Zabel for her work and patience in editing this manuscript. To Diane Wicklund for her encouragement in binding and distributing my sermons for our church family. Your belief in me has been a tremendous encouragement. A special thank you to Janis Eastlund for your editing work before I discovered Grammarly.

To the people of North, I appreciate your love and patience extended to me as your pastor. The gift of Sabbatical made this work possible.

To Brennan, Audrey and Malcolm. I pray for each of you consistently. May God's kingdom take root in your lives so you may produce spiritual fruit.

To my bride – Alyson, thank you for supporting this project. You know me and love me. It's been one of my greatest joys to partner with you in marriage, ministry and parenting.

INTRODUCTION

I told myself I would never travel through Chicago again. Several years ago, we were on our way from Minnesota to Nashville on vacation and went through Illinois en route to our destination. We briefly stopped at the first few toll booths and found we were dropping a dollar at what felt like every mile and a half. We were tempted to pull over and have either my wife or I walk and see who could get through the city faster. Eventually, we discovered a "bill you later" option, so we opted to drive under the cameras and push the expense to a future date. On the return trip, we decided to go around instead of through the big city. It wasn't worth the headache or expense.

We eventually got the bill for our trip (three years after we arrived home). Sometimes in life, it may be beneficial to go around instead of through difficulties.

More often, we must face a problem head-on and press through it. This type of perseverance sounds noble but is counter to my nature. I'm drawn to the path of least resistance. I prefer to be comfortable. I have an app to adjust the thermostat from my recliner and another capable of turning off a lamp five feet from my bed because I'm too lazy to embark on such an arduous journey. The path of least resistance may make for a smoother road but will eventually prevent us from growing in depth. Spiritual substance is formed by going through, not around.

This is especially true in our prayer lives. Superficial conversations lead to superficial friendships. Shallow prayers fail to create a depth of relationship with God. A conversation with God revolving around what we believe He wants to hear instead of what we actually feel may connect us on a surface level but fails to produce intimacy.

Depth is a result of wrestling. Closeness is developed when we work through our questions and doubts, not around them. Truth remains on the surface of our souls when it's collected, stored away and brought back out when opportunities arise for theological discussions. Truth is intended to shape who we are becoming, not simply represent the sum of our spoken beliefs.

Wrestling is an immensely practical exercise critical in producing faith in the life of a believer. It moves us from the theoretical or ideological toward experiencing truth personally. It assists in making that which is true, true of us.

But how do we know if we're making progress? Distance can be measured in steps or miles. Weight is determined by stepping on a scale. Our struggles with God require effort on our part, but progress is difficult to quantify. I've found there are several byproducts produced as we wrestle with God. The fruit of our perseverance (and His grace) is measured by our increased faith and trust in His character and our love for Him and others.

In this pursuit, truth is essential. It becomes a foothold as we press into difficult questions. Unfortunately, for many, the same truth-providing grip may serve as a stop sign for others, halting potential dialogue. We may reason that disagreement with our Creator is disrespectful or dangerous. We may be right. But when we ignore, discount or squash our concerns, we miss an opportunity to discover the "why" behind a directive. We also minimize

God's capacity to handle our deepest doubts and hurt. Truth, as we understand it in scripture, should help prevent us from sinning, not wrestling. Obedience shouldn't be contingent upon our understanding of a commandment. Yet, understanding the heart behind the command is necessary in knowing the one giving us the instruction.

These stop signs extend beyond commands to our beliefs about the Lord. God is good and just, but the evidence in scripture (from a burning bush to the tragedies in Job to various Psalms to the lamentations of the prophets) demonstrates a pattern of questioning the goodness, timing and justice of our Creator. As we navigate this fallen world, instead of seeking to eliminate any vestige of doubt from our minds, we are encouraged to process through it.

When we wrestle with God, we both win. We grow, and He is given glory. It isn't easy. It doesn't come without scars. We may even carry a limp, but as we grapple, the core of who we are begins to change.

This book is broken up into two halves. The first is an invitation to wrestle through questions most of us have regarding prayer. The goal of each chapter isn't to eliminate wrestling by giving conclusive answers. My hope is to invite the reader into a wrestling match with a loving God who desires to be known.

The second half transitions from practical wrestling to practical application. Knowing the need for prayer may create the desire to pray but fails in helping with how it's done. Jesus's disciples knew they were supposed to pray but didn't know how. Jesus responded to their inquiry with the oft-memorized but underutilized outline we often refer to as "The Lord's Prayer." Its structure isn't intended to shape every communication we have with God. Yet, when used as a typical pattern in shaping our prayers, its design helps focus our communication and reorients our lives.

A great deal of ink has been spilled on the topic of prayer. There are books telling stories of corporate prayer's impact on a local church or community. Others focus on listening to God. I've benefited from texts offering practical tools for communicating with God. Some have been written as an indictment on church growth strategies devoid of a prayerful foundation. Some give pragmatic advice on interceding for others.

Every author has a limited canvas to create. No one writer gets to write all the books on prayer. I hope this work will grant the reader permission to wrestle, remove a few stubborn rocks preventing spiritual growth and find in Jesus's outline a structure capable of enhancing and elongating our prayer times.

"Yes, I am the vine; you are the branches. Those who remain in me, and I in them, will produce much fruit. For apart from me you can do nothing." John 15:5

1.

DIFFICULTIES IN PRAYER
IF GOD WANTS US TO PRAY, WHY IS PRAYER SO HARD?

Keep on asking, and you will receive what you ask for. Keep on seeking, and you will find. Keep on knocking, and the door will be opened to you. For everyone who asks, receives. Everyone who seeks, finds. And to everyone who knocks, the door will be opened. You parents—if your children ask for a loaf of bread, do you give them a stone instead? Or if they ask for a fish, do you give them a snake? Of course not! So if you sinful people know how to give good gifts to your children, how much more will your heavenly father give good gifts to those who ask Him.
–Matthew 7:7–11

Prayer is one of the most difficult journeys I have been on in my life. From the moment I first experienced grace, I knew I was supposed to pray.

I remember interceding for my friend who had been abducted by his mother in a messy divorce. For months I had no idea where he was. I remember praying diligently for the Lord to bring him home.

In my youth, I desired an intimate relationship with Christ. I dreamed of having clear feelings and nudges regarding God's plan for my life. In response, I would follow through and do mighty acts for the Lord as part of an epic adventure (often with myself firmly entrenched as the hero in the story).

Difficulties in my plan arose when, in prayer, I failed to discern the difference between a nudge from the Holy Spirit and the effects of spicy chili.

One day God would prompt me to give away a pair of brand-new basketball shoes to a guy who couldn't afford them, which sounded like something He would want.

The next day I'd wake up in the middle of the night, convinced I'd been given the name of my future bride. God forgot to send her the memo.

Additionally complicating my prayer life was my love of spiritual "oooey gooeys." I fell in love with the emotions associated with God's presence. I enjoyed the feeling of being close to God more than I loved God Himself.

I typically felt my prayers were only effective when I could really *feel* my prayers being effective.

I journaled during this time, bemoaning how I must have been the only human in world history experiencing what I was going through.

And all of this before I ever graduated from high school.

I've always believed in the importance of prayer; I've just not always felt the satisfaction that I'm doing it right.

I've yelled at God, shaking my fist at the sky because of my circumstances. Other times, I've avoided addressing issues in my life.

I became comfortable with the giant elephant in the room, praying as if God didn't know what I was hiding. I tried to compartmentalize my prayer life to the point that I could pray about some things (e.g., "Bless my ministry and my family") while ignoring areas of conviction.

I would love to inform the reader that I've exponentially

grown in my prayer life to the point I'm recognized as a spiritual prodigy in the prayer world.

The truth is I want to get better. There are times when I spend over an hour in prayer. However, if we were to distill into parts the content of my prayers, it would include starting on a good note by praising God for who He is. We'd also discover the recitation of the exact requests or patterns of praise I spoke of in my last prayer time with little creativity. I'd then start to think about my day or sports, or I'd begin to wonder how many times the ceiling fan goes around in a minute, or I'd see a speck in the carpet that looked like a face. Then my pocket would vibrate. "Ooo, an email."

In summary, there are days when my prayers look like five minutes of communication with God, thirty minutes of my mind wandering and the remainder of the time spent berating myself about how, as a pastor, I can be so unholy and unable to communicate with God for more than a few minutes.

Prayer is a lot like marriage. We all know it's supposed to be good, but 90 percent of us have significant seasons of struggle with our spouses we'd prefer the rest of the world not know about. But unlike our significant others, the one we communicate with in prayer doesn't currently appear in bodily form. We often can't process our difficulties with others because we're embarrassed and feel we should be doing better as Jesus's followers.

To grow, our silence needs to be brought to light. Nothing good grows in the dark. If prayer is a struggle, the struggle needs to be worked through. The only way we feel isolated in experiencing these difficulties is when we choose to walk through them alone. Bringing them to the surface where they can be exposed allows for progress to be made.

Without vulnerability, we are left to wrestle with uncomfortable questions. For instance, what do we do when we don't like or have a natural affinity toward a deity capable of sending us to hell? The answer is complicated and awkward. So instead, we ignore our condition.

We then spend more time trying to convince ourselves that we are living in a close relationship with God than we spend *in* a close relationship with God.

We face many problems in prayer, but let's start by identifying four of the most common difficulties. (These difficulties are not exhaustive or in any particular order.)

DIFFICULTY 1 – PRAYER IS A GREAT EXPOSER OF OUR DRYNESS AND SPIRITUAL INEPTITUDE

It feels like it shouldn't be this way.

If we approach God and take the time out of our busy schedules to talk to Him, the least He could do is allow a few happy, uplifting feelings to flow through our souls.

Instead, the opposite often occurs. We discover a dryness when we pray. We are exposed when we try to worship God, woodenly reciting phrases we hear in church. Eventually, we transition to where we ask Him about the stuff that really matters to us. God then becomes the procurer of what we want instead of being what we want.

Prayer begins to look like cursing a drinking fountain. We get frustrated with God, blaming Him for our dryness while bemoaning our thirst. Unknowingly, we curse the object capable of quenching our spiritual longings.

One of the great difficulties in prayer is coming to Christ feeling empty. We mistakenly believe we need to manufacture spiritual progress on our end or at least bring a contribution or sacrifice to the table. We assume the need to have a good week managing to surf the internet without fostering a pornography addiction or going a day without yelling at our children. Or, after attending church, we feel better about approaching God. After achieving an elevated level of righteousness, *then* we can pray. This perpetuates the lie that our value and access to God are connected to our behavior.

Hiking out of a spiritual desert will have consequences. The effects of the sun will cause the skin to become dry and brittle. The same is true of our souls. One moisturizing treatment or a long shower won't reverse the sun's damage. It may take time.

The dryness of our prayers may be necessary for fostering the desperation and dependence needed for spiritual breakthroughs.

But this isn't the only difficulty we need to navigate.

DIFFICULTY 2 – FOR SOME, GOD IS NOT OUR HAPPINESS; HE IS A MEANS TO OUR HAPPINESS

In high school, God functioned more like a drug I consumed than a Savior I served. I would get my fix of Jesus at a concert, camp or conference and experience a spiritual high. Unfortunately, after a few weeks, I'd come crashing down when my emotions did what emotions do as a teenager. I would then cry out for the next hit, bemoaning (at times in tears) God's absence.

At the time, I'd yet to come to terms with an

uncomfortable truth. Our deepest longings are connected to our own happiness, which is often the motivation behind our prayers.

Tim Keller's words sting:

> When our heart's treasures seem safe, we don't pray. Seldom do we spend sustained time adoring God. We only pray when circumstances force us. We know God is there, but we tend to see Him as a means through which we get things to make us happy. For most of us, He has not become our happiness. We, therefore, pray to procure things, not know Him better. (Keller, Timothy 2014)

Prayer is intended to develop a relationship. It's not a means of attaining what we want from an uncaring deity.

God wants to do great things for us, but He wants to do them in the context of a relationship where we are speaking to Him as a child addressing a Father. He desires to bless us in a relationship of His choosing, not as a business partnership where we contribute in determining the terms.

We begin the process by asking Him to become our highest affection. "May your name be kept holy" (Matthew 6:9) is not a flowery statement God commands us to pray. It's a practical petition where we daily kick the idols or over-desires of our hearts off the throne intended to be occupied by God alone. Every day we need to reorient our lives around the person who matters most. This is the only path toward making Christ our highest joy.

DIFFICULTY 3 – CAN GOD BE TRUSTED?

Our impeccable Sunday school attendance complicates this question. We know the answer. Yes! God can be trusted. Gold star for you.

Sin exposes us. Every sinful act exposes our failure to believe what He says is true. Our sinful actions communicate that we have life figured out, and our way is better than His. "God, You can bless me, just don't ask me about the way I spend my time, money and talents. Don't deal with the underlying heart sins."

As a religious alternative to prayer, some offer moral behavior devoid of spiritual power or immaculate theological understanding as a substitute for engaging with God over deep-seated sinful patterns.

Dealing with this question is one of the most important we will wrestle with in our faith journey. We will never escape the tension. As long as there is faith to be gained, there will be trust in God's character required.

If we ignore our distrust and doubts, we will not grow. One of my more pivotal moments in life was spent yelling at God regarding my lack of trust in His character.

I found through the process He loved me and could handle my unbelief. He needed to expose it before it could be dealt with. When I was honest regarding my feelings, I gave Him material He could work with.

Placing trust in God is a complicated issue. Many genuine seekers have experienced heart-wrenching events in their lives. "If God is good, how could that happen to me?" "How can I trust a God who would allow _____?" We can each fill in the blank.

Often the blank has kept the seeker from opening their heart to God.

Let me be clear, God doesn't do bad. His provision for human freedom, alongside humanity's fall, each allows for all manner of atrocities to happen in this world. God doesn't promise bad things won't happen, but that when bad things occur, He will be with us. He loves us and will work out even the evil committed against us for His glory and benefit if we allow Him to.

Others live with a warped view of God's sovereignty, which results in a lack of trust. We'll devote an entire chapter to God's control and power, but for this moment, it's essential to remember...

The answer to the question, "Is God good?" was answered in the person of Jesus Christ. Figuring out the complexities surrounding time, eternity, and God's sovereign will are beyond our comprehension and above our pay grades.

In response to this question, God sent His Son who looks like a God, who loves the unlovable, hates pride, and is willing to die on the cross to restore a relationship with humanity. Don't look to a childhood misconception of God. Look to Jesus. He is the fully relatable representation of God every human can understand. Trust Him.

DIFFICULTY 4– IN OUR SIN NATURE, WE ARE WIRED FOR INDEPENDENCE

Some of the first words of a highly capable two-year-old are, "I do it!" That spirit never leaves us, and just like a toddler, this independence often results in chaos, an injury or a mess.

Following Jesus is not an independent pursuit. I once knew a woman whose goal in life was to mature to the point that she didn't need to ask God for anything. Her objective was to be a follower God need not worry about.

Contrast this posture to Jesus, who said, "I tell you the truth, the Son can do nothing by Himself. He does only what He sees the Father doing. Whatever the Father does, the Son also does." – John 5:19

Jesus seems to model a maturity of dependence, not independence.

Prosperity further contributes to this unhealthy independence. The wealthy rely on their talent, resources, and education. Insurance plans and retirement accounts secure our futures. It can be hard to pray, «Give us our daily bread" with a fully-stocked pantry. Even if our soul issues become unbearable, we can find a therapist to assist in dealing with our difficulties on our terms. We then find substitutes for God connected to our control, making prayer difficult.

Paul Miller says this:

> We (Americans) prize accomplishments, production. But prayer is nothing but talking to God. It feels useless as if we are wasting time. Every bone in our body screams, 'Get to work!' When we aren't working, we are used to being entertained. One of the subtlest hindrances to prayer is probably the most pervasive. In the broader culture and in the churches, we prize intellect, competency, and wealth. Because we can do life without God, praying seems nice but unnecessary.

Money can do what prayer does, and it's quicker and less time-consuming. Our trust in ourselves and in our talents makes us structurally independent of God. As a result, exhortations to pray don't stick. (Miller, Paul E. 2017)

This partially explains why, when praying the Lord's Prayer, we are instructed by Jesus to start with God. We begin with our affections and reorder them with Him on top. This needs to happen daily. Outside of spiritual prodigies (and I only know of one), we constantly have idols creeping their way onto the throne of our lives. Because of our flesh, good desires want to become over-desires.

The work God wants to do in us does not come from an independent life but a desperately dependent life. Jesus is clear: "Apart from Me, you can do nothing." Anything of eternal substance is done in His power.

APPLICATION

TRUST THE GOODNESS OF GOD ENOUGH TO OPEN UP TO HIM ABOUT YOUR PRESENT CONDITION

This isn't simply about the act of prayer. Sometimes we focus on our struggles when praying instead of focusing on God Himself. This leads to anxiety. Anxiety and worry then damage our faith and prayer lives.

Paul Miller details the struggle by stating:

What does an unused prayer link look like? Anxiety. Instead of connecting with God, our spirits fly around like severed power lines, destroying everything they touch. Anxiety wants to be God, but lacks God's wisdom, power or knowledge. A God-like stance without God-like character and ability is pure tension. Because anxiety is self on its own, it tries to get control. It is unable to relax in the face of chaos. Once one problem is solved, the next in line steps up. The new one looms so large we forget the last deliverance. (Miller, Paul E. 2017)

Everyone on this planet has a monologue occurring in their heads. Our minds and thoughts produce a script. Often what is produced isn't PG, and if some of the thoughts passing through our minds were made public, we would lose our jobs, the respect of our coworkers and our seats at Thanksgiving dinner. Praise God for a filter most of us possess, enabling only a fraction of what is thought to escape our lips.

The monologue in our heads was initially intended to be a dialogue.

Praying without ceasing doesn't entail constantly reciting prayers but simply inviting a Father who desires to bless us into the conversation already taking place in our minds. Allow His words to help in decision-making. He is a Father who wants to give good gifts, but the best gift is a relationship with Himself. We must remain in Him, not simply occasionally visit.

Approach God honestly. He can take our messiness and even our weak desires and begin to work with them. He is big enough to receive our angry thoughts about Him and listen without thinking less of us. If we repeatedly come into His presence and listen to Him through His Word, we will find Him faithful in revealing His character and extending His love toward us over time. When this happens, we find these four difficulties begin to lessen in our lives.

2.

THE IMPORTANCE OF PRAYER
DOES PRAYER MAKE A DIFFERENCE?

And you are helping us by praying for us. Then
many people will give thanks because God
has graciously answered so many prayers
for our safety. –2 Corinthians 1:11

Prayer is an important activity. God tells us it matters, but at times we may still question its necessity in our lives. We can drift into thinking that if God wants an event to occur, He's more than capable of doing it Himself. An entity powerful enough to create the entire universe by simply speaking it into existence is more than capable of doing whatever He wants. Why should I then pray or ask Him for anything?

The answers are found throughout the pages of scripture.

Paul saw a direct correlation between his ministry success and the prayers of the churches he served. Peter, in his epistle, encouraged Christ-followers to be earnest and disciplined in their prayers.

Jesus consistently spent time alone with His Father. He later interceded on Peter's behalf. Immediately, before the disciple would disown Him, He told him, "Simon, Simon, Satan has asked to sift each of you like wheat. But I have pleaded in prayer for you, Simon, that your faith should not fail. So when you have repented and turned to me again, strengthen your brothers." –Luke 22:31–32

Why would Jesus pray for something so specific? Why not simply trust God's will be done and move on?

Christ lived as if prayer mattered. Before choosing His disciples, He spent an entire night praying about the decision. He remains our best example of how we should live our lives, alongside modeling the importance of prayer.

Regardless of our views on the sovereignty of God, the posture modeled in scripture emphasizes the importance of prayer.

However, an example in prayer doesn't answer an important question. Why is it important to pray?

An exhaustive list would undoubtedly be longer, but I'll mention three reasons prayer is essential in the life of a believer.

REASON 1– GOD DELIGHTS IN USING OUR HANDS TO DO HIS WORK

Watchman Nee says the following, which initially makes me uncomfortable:

> God is omnipotent, but He needs a channel on earth before He can manifest His omnipotence. We cannot increase God's power, but we can hinder His power. Man cannot increase God's power, but he can block His power. We cannot ask God to do what He does not want to do, but we can limit what He wants to do. (Nee, Watchman 1995)

He interprets the verse in scripture, "I tell you the truth, whatever you forbid on earth will be forbidden in heaven, and whatever you permit on earth will be permitted in heaven." (Matthew 18:18) to mean there must be a move on earth before there is a move in heaven. He believes that, in Christ, great authority has been given to the church to move Heaven to act.

Part of my struggle with his statement is connected to the nature of God's salvation. His deliverance is not portrayed this way in scripture. When the Israelites were in slavery, God did the complete work. The Hebrew slaves contributed nothing other than their trust. In faithful obedience, they applied the blood to their doorposts. They were not tasked to perform a single plague.

The same is true of Jesus. He delivered us without any work on our behalf. Again, the only application comes in faith, confessing our sins and allowing His blood to cover our transgressions. We receive His righteousness as a gift.

However, after deliverance from Egypt, God wanted the Israelites to learn trust and obedience. Through the sacrificial system, they were reminded of what was necessary to approach God. In response, they were to pray in order to bring about the fullness of His will in their lives.

The same is true in the New Testament. A Christ-follower is never called to work *for* their salvation but told to work *out* their salvation. Prayer is the primary act in which this work begins to happen.

Philip Yancey puts it this way:

We are Christ's body on earth. After all, He has no hands but ours. And yet to act as Christ's body we need unbroken, connection to the Head. We pray in order to see the world with God's eyes, and then join the stream of power as it breaks loose. (Yancey, Philip 2006)

In the New Testament, God never describes Himself as separate from us. We are living stones being built into a spiritual temple. Christ is the cornerstone of the structure. We are united as one body with Christ as the head. We are His hands and feet.

When connected to the head, His Spirit will initiate and prompt us, but we are still encouraged to act obediently on the impulses. Apart from the work of salvation, He will not act for us.

His empowerment comes through prayer. Many in the church fail to experience victory in their lives because they've failed in consistently asking Him for it.

As the church is connected and dependent upon Christ the Head, we are then free to move into the world with His power capable of accomplishing His desires.

We have been given a great resource in this world and are encouraged by Jesus to use the authority found in His name to ask and receive.

This isn't a magical incantation using Jesus's name to get whatever fleshly desire we want. Instead, we should ask because Jesus acted, and the early church acted like heaven could and should be moved by earth.

If this is true, prayer should be a priority in our lives.

Andrew Murray says, "Prayer must not be looked at

as a means of maintaining our own Christian life. It is the highest part of the work entrusted to us." (Murray, Andrew 1885)

God has chosen prayer as a means to establish His kingdom on earth. I don't believe God desires to see injustice, arrogance, and violence in the world. I'm confident He doesn't want to see people created in His image live lives apart from His power. These tragedies continue to occur partly because the church has not consistently asked Him to do anything about it.

Because Jesus modeled it, I believe we are to live out of a posture that prayer moves the power of God toward earth to do His kingdom work.

REASON 2– PRAYER MAKES IT SAFE FOR GOD TO GIVE US MANY OF THE THINGS WE MOST DESIRE

If I were a billionaire, I would enjoy giving my kids a million dollars. After careful consideration, I would then abstain from this act of generosity because they wouldn't know what to do with it. If I did, our family would end up with a vacation home near an amusement park with a vast assortment of Nerf guns, gaming systems, and Lego sculptures. It would be detrimental for me to bless their greatest desires.

Prayer is often a revealer of our greatest desires.

I had a good desire as a young man. I wanted to be married. It's a natural desire, even a biblical desire. When a man finds a wife, he finds a good thing. From the moment girls dropped their cooties, I was a man on a mission. The desire occupied a great deal of my prayer life. It's what I focused on. Honestly, it was a good gift I had made an idol in my life.

This didn't stop me from praying for this over-inflated good thing. I obsessed. I grew up in a church convinced the end was near, so while everyone else was pleading, "Come, Lord Jesus," I was praying, "Could You just wait until after my honeymoon?" I wrote letters to my future wife as a fourteen-year-old boy. I remember only one line from these love notes. "And when our hands join together, they will form a bond so strong not even the power of hell will break it." Graciously, my mother inadvertently threw them away.

My desires had a veneer of faithfulness. They hinted at godliness, but they became the most important pursuit of my life. God had become a means to an end. He was a means to my happiness. If I were to grow old and alone, He was destined to be a consolation prize, not my greatest joy.

The same prayer exposing me ultimately changed me. In my communication with God, wrestling with Him, and, to be honest, yelling at Him, I came to experience a significant transformation in my life. Through my asking, He changed me.

He changed my heart and exposed the shadow I was chasing. He revealed Himself as the substance of my heart's desire. I'm summing up fifteen years of struggle and prayer into a few words in a chapter of a book, but the end result was greater trust in Jesus and His plan for my life. He changed me to the point I could be blessed with a wife.

Prayer is the place where God can safely give us what we ask for. When we come to Him and ask, even if it's a selfish ask detrimental to our long-term good, it provides an opportunity for Him to work and begin to give us His best yes. It creates an avenue of communication.

His silence forces me to ask questions when what I'm asking for isn't happening. It forces me to wrestle with the character of God and His plans for my life.

I used to get embarrassed when I reflected on my selfish and immature prayers, but now instead see them as instruments God used to work within me His desires for my life. He already knew my deepest longings. Contrasting my warped desires with His will revealed in scripture exposed a disconnect but also created a dependency in me. I was invited to rely on His power to change my behaviors, thoughts and motives.

At the beginning of this process, I often felt God was hesitant to answer my prayers. In hindsight, His hesitancy was tied to my asking for things that would gratify my flesh or improve my circumstances, not develop my character. As I've grown and pushed through in honesty with God, I've learned along with Martin Luther that, "Prayer is not overcoming God's reluctance. It is laying hold of God's willingness."

Prayer is important because it changes the world we live in but is also imperative because it changes us.

REASON 3– PRAYER MOVES THE IMPLICATIONS OF THE GOSPEL INTO OUR EVERYDAY EXPERIENCE

When we believe the Gospel and become reconciled with God, we are immediately declared holy and blameless as we stand before Him without a single fault. (Colossians

1:22) This is our unchangeable position. It is the gift of God through Christ.

And for a couple of weeks, we feel this way. Upon receiving Christ, we experience an incredibly joyful season. Where our lives once produced thorns and weeds, we are now capable of producing fruit.

I have an apple tree in my front yard. In Minnesota, the tree produces small pink flowers during the three days of spring. It's a lovely sight. New life is beautiful, but it's not fruit. We can't eat flowers. The pedals get stuck in our teeth. A harvest takes time, and fruit is only produced when the root system is healthy and receives nutrients from the soil.

One of the initial struggles a new believer faces is the loss of their flowers, but without the loss, the fruit will not form. Spiritually speaking, fruit is more important than flowers.

So how does fruit form? How does the righteousness of Christ become a maturing reality in the life of the believer? Jesus tells us in John 15:

> Yes, I am the vine; you are the branches. Those who remain in me, and I in them, will produce much fruit. For apart from me you can do nothing… But if you remain in me and my words remain in you, you may ask for anything you want, and it will be granted! When you produce much fruit, you are my true disciples. This brings great glory to my father. —John 15:5, 7–8

Fruit is connected to a growing relationship with Jesus

Christ where we listen to God by reading His Word and then praying for His power to live under His rule.

Incredibly, Jesus encourages us to ask. When we are confronted with an issue in our lives or exposed as less than we know we're supposed to be, we shouldn't hide in darkness. Instead, our struggle should be brought to the light. We are to ask God to work His righteousness in us.

As a pastor, I have a propensity toward pride. If attendance is up, I must be doing something right. I can drift into thinking of myself as better than others, more holy than others, and I can't stand it when others point out something wrong in my life. All of this finds its origin in pride, and at times it feels overwhelming.

Thankfully, God encourages me in His Word to ask and keep on asking. I'm not insinuating that a three-week commitment to prayer has resulted in pride being completely eradicated from my life, never to be seen again. What it does mean is that part of the fruit of the Spirit, humility, will begin to ripen in my life. Prayer is directly connected to spiritual growth.

Tim Keller says this about prayer and discipleship:

> Prayer is the way that all the things we believe in and that Christ has won for us actually become our strength. Prayer is the way that truth is worked into your heart to create new instincts, reflexes and dispositions. (Keller, Timothy 2014)

It takes time (in fact, a lifetime) to see it all work out, but God promises it will. Anything we need to please God and become more like Him is available to us as we ask

Him for it. This is part of why Paul is so adamant about continual prayer.

APPLICATION
SET ASIDE TIME TO PRAY

Andrew Murray says: "Those who do not have a set time to pray, do not pray."(Murray, Andrew 1885)

If we want to experience these three realities, we need to start praying. It may feel unnatural. We may be tempted to start with flowery language we think God might want to hear. Instead, we simply bring ourselves. Feel free to allow the mind to wander and then bring it back under the umbrella of His grace.

Be intentional. Listen to His words by reading the scripture and then honestly respond to the text. God isn't turned away by thoughts that aren't perfectly sanctified. He's more interested in us.

Philip Yancey quoted Henri Nouwen, who said after his own journey in prayer that, "Sitting in the presence of God for one hour each morning – day after day, week after week, and month after month in total confusion and with a myriad of distractions – radically changed my life."(Yancey, Philip 2006)

To grow, we need to be intentional and set aside time to be with God.

3.

JESUS'S EXAMPLE IN PRAYER
WHAT CAN JESUS'S PRAYER LIFE
TEACH US ABOUT OUR OWN?

> Before daybreak the next morning, Jesus got up and
> went out to an isolated place to pray. —Mark 1:35

As I've grown older, I've become convinced I had it right in kindergarten.

We went to Sunday School every week. I learned the stories of the Bible on flannelgraph.

We earned shiny gold, silver, green, blue or red stars for attendance each week and maybe an extra if we memorized a verse or for good behavior. We sang the classics like, "The B.I.B.L.E.," "Jesus Loves Me," and everyone's favorite: the "Arky Arky" song (YouTube it).

We earned awards, certificates, and the holy grail of all prizes: a full-size candy bar as our sticker chart filled up.

I recall learning lessons on sharing, which were immediately followed by arguments over the best toys in the toy box.

What I remember most during these formative years is when asked a question, if you didn't know the answer, you should always say, "Jesus."

It has four legs, wears a collar, and barks. It may sound like a dog, but you better go with "Jesus" just to be safe.

Over time we mature and develop minds capable of thinking in more nuanced and complex ways.

However, as I grow older, I've begun to realize Jesus is the answer to more questions than I previously dreamed possible.

How do I know God loves me? The answer is Jesus. Is there any way God can accept me knowing what I've done? The answer is found in Jesus.

Jesus is the face of God the Father on earth. And we need a face.

When writing letters or emailing another person, we're limited by our inability to see a face. I may read what a person says, but without their expressions, I might interpret what they say in ways they never intended to communicate.

This is true in our messaging. I'm a forty-six-year-old man who occasionally uses an emoji when I send a text. My mother is a fan of emojis in my family group chats.

Why do we find it necessary to exchange simple cartoon faces with one another? We subconsciously understand the importance of sending a face to communicate what we're feeling and how we desire the conversation to be received.

Jesus is the face of God and the heart of God expressed in human form. As a result, He then becomes our guide in teaching us how we should relate to the Father. If we want to know how to pray, we must look to Him as our model. When we observe how He prayed and even struggled in prayer, our communication with God can then be shaped by His example.

We start with dependency.

JESUS TOOK A PLACE OF DEPENDENCE
WHILE HE WALKED AMONG US

Our natural instinct is to find an identity apart from God. Adam and Eve began this quest when they chose the Tree of the Knowledge of Good and Evil over the Tree of Life. Instead of finding their life in God and His presence, they chose to usurp His role, establishing their own set of rights and wrongs. They wanted to determine how life should work outside of the way God ordained it to work.

Humanity has been a mess ever since.

Jesus modeled a much different posture.

He said, "When you have lifted up the Son of Man on the cross, then you will understand that I am he. I do nothing on my own but say only what the father taught me." –John 8:28

Jesus, before the creation of time, was God. He could say a word and that word had the power to create substance. "Let there be light," (Genesis 1:3) and there was. Jesus had and currently has this power. But as Philippians 2 reminds us, He emptied Himself of His divine privileges and took the humble position of a slave and was born as a human being. –Philippians 2:7

Paul Miller contrasts Jesus's posture with Adam and Eve's:

> Adam and Eve began their quest for self-identity after the fall. Only after they acted independently of God did they have a sense of separate self. Because Jesus has no separate sense of self, He has no identity

crisis, no angst. Consequently, He doesn't try to find Himself. He knows Himself only in relationship with the Father. (Miller, Paul E. 2017)

I understand a desire for self-sustainability. I don't like being dependent upon anyone. I could borrow half of the tools I need for a project because I rarely use them due to my lack of discernible man skills. However, I would rather be thirty dollars poorer than rely on my neighbor. In contrast, I'm more than willing to be generous with what I own and loan it out freely.

The reason I struggle reciprocating is rooted in unhealthy independence. If we aren't careful, this same over-desire for autonomy bleeds into our relationship with God.

I don't want to rely on Him for my emotional stability because it requires trust in His character. I hesitate in bringing Him my real problems because it forces me to deal with my own deep-seated issues. Faith requires relinquishing control.

If I allow Him access to my pain, there is no guarantee He won't expose other tender places, but when we do, we realize…

Jesus isn't asking us to do anything He isn't already doing. He is inviting us into His life, a helpless dependence on His heavenly Father. To become more like Jesus is to feel increasingly unable to do life, increasingly wary of your heart. Paradoxically, you get holier while you are feeling unholy. The very thing you are trying to escape – your inability – opens the door to prayer and then grace. (Miller, Paul E. 2017)

If we don't pursue and embrace our dependence upon God, we will never grow in our prayer lives.

We also learn…

JESUS PRAYED EVEN IN THE MIDST OF A BUSY LIFE

"After sending them home, He went up into the hills by Himself to pray. Night fell while He was there alone." –Matthew 14:23

"One day soon afterward Jesus went up on a mountain to pray, and He prayed to God all night." –Luke 6:12

When faced with a major decision, Jesus went away and prayed. After spending extended time with people, Jesus desired to be alone with His Father. At times He was interrupted and had mercy on the crowds, but it was His habit to get away and pray.

Jesus was busy, but His heart remained at peace.

When we refuse to pray, we communicate to God that our circumstances are under control. Our power is sufficient for the task at hand. Jesus modeled the opposite.

JESUS WASN'T AFRAID TO PRAY FOR BIG THINGS

I am praying not only for these disciples but also for all who will ever believe in me through their message. I pray that they will all be one, just as you and I are one— as you are in me, Father, and I am in you. And may they be in us so that the world will believe you sent me. I have given them the glory you gave me, so they may be one as we are one. I am in them and you are in me. May they experience such perfect unity that the world will know that you sent me and that you love them as much as you love me. —John 17:20–23

Jesus, in this text, is not praying specifically for His original twelve disciples. He is praying for those who will come to know Him as a result of their message. Let's recap the main thrust of His prayer — that "they may be one, just as you and I are one."

Describing the Trinity is difficult. Eggs, the three forms of water, three-in-one shampoo and three-leaf clovers fail to explain the complexity of the Godhead. Where does the Father start and the Son end, and how does the Holy Spirit fit in? They are so interconnected, the human mind cannot fathom pulling them apart without drifting into heresy.

Yet, in this text, we have Jesus praying that we will share this same unity as believers. Jesus is praying for human beings to experience Trinitarian unity with one another.

Most of us experience unity because we refuse to talk in-depth with one another. Churches split over carpet color, the length of a pastor's prayer and disagreements over timelines regarding the end of the world. I've heard of board meetings growing heated regarding whether the church should adopt two-ply or three-ply toilet paper or lengthy discussions over purchasing a Bunn coffeemaker due to how close it sounds to the word "butt." The moment we move toward meaningful relationships, the result is often friction. Jesus prayed a big prayer that will not be fully answered until we arrive in heaven, but it didn't prevent Him from praying for it while He was on earth.

He's praying for the full and complete application of our new Gospel reality. His boldness should, in turn, give us boldness in praying for an addiction, a sinful behavioral pattern or more grace in a relationship with a spouse. God's answer to our prayers may not be given as a simple "yes" or "no" but instead come in incremental growth. We should see what God wants and boldly pray that it will become a reality in our lives and community. Our difficulties in intercession rarely occur because we pray for things too difficult for God.

More often, our requests are too small. We fail to take hold of the power available to us in Christ to do far more than we could ever ask or imagine.

FOR JESUS, PRAYER WAS THE PLACE TO STRUGGLE

It's common for us to catch ourselves in prayer saying, "Lord, I trust You," but even as we say the words, we know they aren't true.

We assume prayer and trust go hand in hand. As a result, we may incorrectly deduce we need to achieve a certain level of faith before we approach God with a request.

This wasn't how Jesus modeled prayer. He certainly trusted the Father, but this trust did not eliminate wrestling with His father in prayer. Prayer is a place Jesus struggled.

Haddon Robbinson made this point:

> For most of us, prayer serves as a resource to help in times of testing or conflict. For Jesus it was the battle itself. Once the

Gethsemane prayers had aligned Him with the Father's will, what happened next was merely a means to fulfill it. Prayer mattered much.

Where was it that Jesus sweat great drops of blood? Not in Pilate's Hall, nor on His way to Golgotha. It was the garden of Gethsemane. There He offered up prayers and petitions with loud cries and tears to the one who could save Him from death. Had I witnessed that struggle I would have been worried about the future. If He is so broken up when all He is doing is praying, I might have said, 'What will He do when He faces a real crisis? Why can't He approach this ordeal with the calm confidence of His sleeping friends?' Yet when the test came, Jesus walked to the cross with courage, and His friends fell apart and fell away. (Haddon W. Robbinson; Dave Branon 2016)

For Jesus, His struggle was a natural desire to avoid crucifixion and separation from His Father. There is nothing sinful about the desire, but through prayer, Jesus grappled with the Father's will for salvation.

For us to pray as God wants us to pray, we can't give up wrestling in prayer. Hitting a roadblock or confronting an out-of-whack desire is not the time to quit or wait until we get better. It's an opportunity to wrestle with God in authenticity with where we are currently. We should be honest, bringing our struggles to Him.

Jesus walked Golgotha in strength because He

wrestled privately in prayer. The same must be true of us. Struggles should drive us to prayer. We should persevere through a trial until we share God's heart toward our circumstances and commit to faithful obedience.

PRAYER REMAINS A PRIORITY TO JESUS

"But because Jesus lives forever, His priesthood lasts forever. Therefore, He is able, once and forever, to save those who come to God through Him. He lives forever to intercede with God on their behalf." –Hebrews 7:24–25

"Who dares accuse us whom God has chosen for His own? No one—for God Himself has given us right standing with Himself. Who then will condemn us? No one—for Christ Jesus died for us and was raised to life for us, and He is sitting in the place of honor at God's right hand, pleading for us." –Romans 8:33–34

"My dear children, I am writing this to you so that you will not sin. But if anyone does sin, we have an advocate who pleads our case before the father. He is Jesus Christ, the one who is truly righteous." –1 John 2:1

Jesus and the Father are one. When we see the Son, we have seen the heart of the Father. Therefore, the intercession of Christ is not Jesus the Son begging at the feet of God the Father for requests outside His will.

In His intercession, this is the resurrected Jesus, becoming our high priest. He has covered our sins. He now lives for our sanctification. He is still working and praying on our behalf.

The Holy Spirit also works for our benefit. scripture says that when we don't know how to pray, the Spirit intercedes on our behalf with groans that our words cannot express. (Romans 8:27) He prayed on our behalf on earth and hasn't stopped in His resurrected state. This should comfort us as we wrestle and struggle in our relationship with God.

APPLICATION

FIND VALUE IN A RELATIONSHIP WITH GOD AND A NEW IDENTITY IN CHRIST

Jesus is our great example in prayer, but before we follow Him as an example, we must first embrace a new identity. Our identification with His work on our behalf is foundational to following the patterns He set in prayer.

Often we connect our peace with our circumstances: "My life is going well. I received a promotion or pay raise at my job. People seem to genuinely like me. My kids are on the honor role. My wife and I have been getting along of late."

If peace is external, any change in circumstance can then rob us of our peace.

Jesus modeled an identity defined by who He was in relation to the Father. As a result, when His best friends slept while He was sweating drops of blood, He remained secure. Or, when He witnessed thousands of people abandon Him or was betrayed by one of His closest friends, He remained at peace.

If Jesus's security was defined by His external circumstances, He would have lost any semblance of peace. But instead, He was inwardly defined by His relationship with the Father.

Before we find value in any methodology, example or

outline (even if the outline is laid out by Jesus Himself), the foundation of effective prayer is built on a proper understanding of our identity in Christ.

We follow Christ's example only to the degree we embrace our standing as God's adopted children through His Son's work.

4.

PRAYER AND THE SOVEREIGNTY OF GOD
WHY PRAY WHEN GOD'S IN CONTROL OF EVERYTHING?

And we know that God causes everything to work together for the good of those who love God and are called according to His purpose for them. –Romans 8:28

My college years were formative for my spiritual journey. There, I was exposed to and wrestled with various faith experiences and differing theological views.

I was a Baptist kid who grew up with revivals and sermons ending with altar calls spoken over the top of the third verse of a closing hymn. In my elementary years, we examined the moral implications of nearly every famous PG-rated story in the Bible. As a teenager, we focused on the issues that mattered most, like "how far is too far" in a dating relationship, saying no to drugs and alcohol, peer pressure, and the book of Revelation.

I went to a Presbyterian liberal arts school. The college was conservative as a whole, but it was there I first interacted with liberal theology. I had other friends desperate for me to be filled with the Holy Ghost, specifically speaking in tongues. I'd driven by Catholic churches but never talked to an actual Catholic about what they believed. So, I wrestled.

True to its Reformed roots, in short order, I was introduced to people who considered themselves Calvinists. There were five-point, three-point and a few who added a point or two, adhering to a seven-point version of John Calvin's teaching. They spoke in the language of TULIPS. My grandma grew tulips. They were pretty, but I had no idea this flower was an acronym for aspects of a specific systematic theology. It was all very confusing for a guy who just wanted to see people saved.

I was exposed to the doctrines of God's election and predestination. I was shown scriptures pointing toward God's sovereign choice and what looked like the predetermination of who's in and who's out.

While my classmates were out enjoying life and dating, I was in my dorm room pondering the deep questions of life, and it quickly became a crisis of faith.

I began to spiral.

Can God be God without infinite knowledge of how world events will conclude?

Does He genuinely care for everyone or just the elect?

Am I capable of making a decision, or is all of life determined and set in stone? Are we puppets playing out a drama with invisible strings controlling our choices with only the illusion of free will?

If God is in control, why do bad things happen? If He dictates human history, how can those who have never been exposed to the Good News be held accountable for a message they have never heard?

And relevant for these writings - how am I then supposed to pray?

I'd summarize my collegiate prayers with the following:

"Dear Jesus, I pray you will do the things you want to do that I ultimately have no control over. I ask that the things you have already predetermined and set in stone will remain set in stone. I suppose they are already set in stone, so I'm not sure why I'm praying in the first place. So, Lord, I hope you planned before the beginning of time to make a highly attractive girl in the other dorm fall in love with me. Bless my family. Amen."

The implications of a warped view of the sovereignty of God can wreck a prayer life alongside our intimacy with God.

The foundational question at the heart of this wrestling remains a stumbling block for many: "Is God good, and does He care?"

So, I prayed. I brought my struggles to Jesus and asked Him to show me what to make of all these questions. This chapter is the result of many years of struggle.

I'll start with a discouraging statement. We are incapable of fully grasping the answers to these questions as a part of fallen humanity. We'd have better luck teaching the family cat trigonometry than figuring out the mystery of God's sovereign will.

A posture of humility is the only safe context to work through these issues.

Throughout the pages of scripture, we find the sovereignty of God isn't a doctrine to be feared but one to be encouraged by. A proper posture in prayer should be enhanced, not hindered, by God's control over history.

Let's begin with what we know from scripture.

GOD LOOKS FOR PARTNERS TO WORK WITH

From the beginning of time, God has seen His relationship with created human beings as a partnership. He set up the garden and established parameters allowing it to flourish. He created everything to work well but then commanded Adam and Eve to go and subdue it.

He desired to see what they would do with the creativity He gave them. They had options. There were choices in naming the animals and how they would arrange and work the garden. God didn't micromanage.

He could have created the world to be self-sustaining, where humanity didn't need to plant and harvest food to survive. He could have made a world independent of human work or effort.

After the fall, God was still looking for a partner. He pulled Abraham out of his home, called Moses through a bush, and used Samson despite his uncontrolled lust. God was looking for someone to work through and with.

Phillip Yancey says:

> History is the story of God giving away power. After entrusting the human species with the gift of free choice, God invited its representatives to act as partners, even to argue and wrestle with the One who created them. Yet virtually everyone God picked to lead a new venture — Adam, Abraham, Moses, David — proved disappointing in part. Apparently, God committed to work with human partners no matter how inept. (Yancey, Philip 2006)

In the New Testament, God did a similar work. He didn't assign the gospel presentation to angels or leave us with an additional tablet handwritten by the finger of God. Even scripture was composed as a partnership between the Holy Spirit and human hands.

God is still in search of partners. The will of humanity continues to make up a part of the equation regarding God's control. His people work in the power of His Spirit to tend the garden and bring about kingdom fruitfulness in the places He has called them to work.

This truth makes an occupation (not just the work done for Jesus within the church) more meaningful. Because God has called His people to a new work, bringing about His kingdom rule into all aspects of a daily grind is now possible. This extends beyond leading coworkers to Christ. It entails being an honest salesman, the hardest worker on a construction crew, or a servant leader. We bring God's kingdom ethic wherever He places us. If we fail, an angel isn't going to be dispatched and do it for us.

This is how God has created our planet to work. It's because...

GOD HAS AN INCREDIBLE RESPECT FOR HUMAN FREEDOM

C.S. Lewis, in an essay entitled "Work and Prayer," puts it this way:

> Why wash your hands? If God intends for them to be clean, they'll come clean without your washing them...Why ask for salt? Why put on your boots? Why do anything? God

could have arranged things so that our bodies nourished themselves miraculously without food, knowledge entered our brains without studying, umbrellas naturally appeared to protect us from rain storms. God chose a different style of governing the world, a partnership which relies on human agency and choice. (Yancey, Philip 2006)

This dynamic is motivated by love. There is no love without choice. It was a risk when God created a people in His image. Love must be chosen.

This explains, in part, the presence of two trees in the garden. It's why, after Jesus died for the sins of all humanity, salvation is still something to be accepted or rejected. He will not force us to follow Him against our will.

I'm not sure how God's choosing of us completely works, but in reading scripture, I've come to believe that however it occurs, it doesn't completely usurp human free will.

GOD IS UNCHANGEABLE, BUT SOME OF HIS PLANS CAN CHANGE

Malachi 3:6 says, "I, the Lord, do not change."

Hosea 11:18 reads: "My heart is changed within me; all my compassion is aroused."

Or maybe you've heard this from Numbers 2:19: "God is not a man, so He does not lie. He is not human, so He does not change His mind. Has He ever spoken and failed to act? Has He ever promised and not carried it through?"

In context, the last verse describes an instance where

a world leader was attempting to bribe a prophet of God to curse the people of God and was willing to pay the prophet handsomely for his services.

When God chooses people as His own, He doesn't change His mind.

In other instances, we see God willing to be adaptable to His servants' requests. He communicated through a prophet to King Hezekiah the need to get his affairs in order because he would soon die. Hezekiah responds by begging for a little more time, and God grants him additional years.

Abraham negotiates and pleads with God on behalf of wicked Sodom and Gomorrah. God concedes and honors the patriarch's request.

A tension exists between a God who is both sovereign over human history and engaged and adaptable in a live interaction with His creation.

Though the dynamic is hard to understand, it is clear from scripture that humanity's response to the tension is not inaction. The sovereignty of God is never intended to lead to passivity in humanity. Even in moments where God displays His power devoid of human effort, there is still an expected response from those who witness these acts.

The pages of scripture are filled with wrestling and ongoing arguments between God and His people.

Even the metaphors God uses to describe Himself are adaptable images.

God portrays Himself as a potter (He forms), creator (He is both architect and designer), nurturer (mother with child, a hen with chicks), and gardener (He keeps a vineyard and adapts to make it productive and fruitful).

Creation is ongoing. Jesus describes His Father as always at work, even to this day.

We mistakenly view the created order as static. On the cross, Jesus said, "It is finished." (John 19:30) In creation, He said, "It is very good." (Genesis 1:31) There is still work to be done.

I've had a conversation with a neighbor who is both a Christ-follower and a potter. He described today's ceramic work as much different than pottery created in ancient history due to modern refining processes. In ancient Israeli history, being a potter required adaptability. The clay could be stubborn and not cooperate with the original intention for the piece. As a result, the potter was forced to work and re-form the piece in response to the pliability of the clay.

This is an important truth regarding prayer. Sometimes, our Heavenly Father may need to work around our stubbornness and inflexibility. Growth involves wrestling with Him and asking for circumstances misaligned with His purposes to be subdued and brought under Christ's rule. It means we must also remain flexible as we process through the answers He gives to our prayers.

IT'S NOT ABOUT ANSWERING A QUESTION. IT'S ABOUT DEVELOPING A PROPER POSTURE

There is a hard truth associated with this discussion. An infant has a greater chance of designing, building and then piloting a rocket ship into space than we have of thoroughly understanding the depth of God's sovereign work in human history.

I'll illustrate.

Imagine God putting His kids in a massive amusement park where every ride produces and instills the different character qualities of the park's creator within the souls of His children.

There are rides producing love; others develop patience, self-control and gentleness. There are rides including suffering. They don't have long lines, but those who experience them are often grateful.

The more a child participates, the more they grow.

In the middle of the park is a playground. It's central and can be seen from any ride. The playground represents the sovereignty of God. It serves as a reminder of God's overarching plans, power and purposes.

The playground looks like a blast, but when kids approach the gate, they are confronted by a colorful measuring stick and an arrow. Some kids try wearing high-heeled shoes or standing on their tippy toes, but no matter how high they stretch, every child in the park fails to reach the height requirement.

In a real-life scenario, an authority would be in place to prevent any overanxious child from sneaking into the playground. Unbelievably, in this scenario, there isn't an angel with a fiery sword preventing kids from climbing on the equipment. The kids can go in, and, unfortunately, many have.

After spending time swinging on the swings and sliding down a few slides, those who spend time on the inside exit with more knowledge than they began with. They might explain to other kids how Jesus only died for the elect. While crossing a rope bridge, they encountered two lenses God uses to view the world. Through one, He is burdened for all of humanity; with the other, He receives glory and finds delight even in sending people to hell.

This sets poorly with others who, up to this point, had been perfectly content riding the other rides. In response, they go in themselves to prove the other guy wrong. They play on the same toys, swing on the same swings, and twirl on the same merry-go-rounds, yet describe a much different experience. They suggest God doesn't know what's coming next in human history. He directs circumstances for His eternal ends but is just as surprised as we are as history unfolds.

The end result of this pursuit looks similar to a toddler playing on equipment not designed for them. It's dangerous. They may get bloody, invite others to join them, and their experiences cause pain and confusion in other children who should be enjoying the rides intended for their growth.

God's sovereignty is intended to bring us comfort as we ride the ups and downs of this life. In suffering and trial, knowing the playground exists is essential, even if we fail to understand completely how it operates. We will someday grow tall enough to explore and celebrate a plan and purpose beyond our understanding, but not until we graduate from this life and enter the next.

We may still ask questions. "Is God good?" "Does prayer matter?" The answers have been given to us, but not through a full explanation of God's sovereign work. Jesus is undoubtedly our example in prayer. But He is also much more.

JESUS IS THE ANSWER TO ANY QUESTION REGARDING GOD'S SOVEREIGN LOVE

I settled a few years ago into what I believe is a proper posture toward the sovereignty of God. Faith, in its essence, is a belief in the unseen. There are facets and variables of God's plan hidden from me. I believe God hides aspects of His will because I'm easily distracted.

I've grown to understand my faith is meant to be placed in a person, not a plan.

Just because I can't see everything doesn't mean my faith is blind. It's a revealed trust. When we've seen Jesus, we've seen the heart of the Father. He is our great example, but He is also the answer to the question, "Does God care?" He is the relatable face of the Father. In Him, we see the emotion of God.

We can't completely understand cosmic warfare, the battle in the heavenly realms, and how it affects humanity, but we can relate to Jesus. I can't provide a comprehensive answer to why bad things happen, but I can trust who I see in the Gospels as the Savior of the world.

We may still wonder about a variety of questions. What do we do with all the people who have never heard the Gospel, those who haven't had an opportunity to respond to messages others hear weekly in church? Is God loving? What happens to the abused child who grew up to be an abusive father who parented a child who also became an abusive father? How is this scenario fair when others have parents who love them? All of this is beyond me.

I can't answer every why and what if, but I can point to the only person in human history I trust to judge fairly. The man who loved the prostitute and tax collector, who made every way possible for the broken to come to Him, is capable of judging the world.

God answered the question of His sovereignty with more clarity than we often assume. He sent His Son to show us the full expression of the Godhead in a relatable human form. And then encouraged us to trust in His love and sacrifice for our salvation.

Let's examine a few implications of these truths.

APPLICATION

BELIEF IN THE SOVEREIGNTY OF GOD SHOULD RESULT IN:

HOPE

When wrestling through issues surrounding the sovereignty of God, the end result should be hope. If it's not, there is still more wrestling to be done. The God of the Bible was revealed in the person of Jesus Christ. He suffered more than any human being will ever suffer. Yet a new hope was born through what appeared to be the world's greatest tragedy. The Gospel is the great softener of the human heart. Whether spoken or its implications lived out, it is the power to soften hardened clay.

This hope is foundational to our growth as followers of Christ. It gives us stamina in praying through times of suffering and difficulty.

When hope is gone, we dull ourselves with religious lives. We try hard to do what God wants apart from an intimate relationship with Him. A proper posture of God's sovereignty may allow for wrestling regarding the purpose of a trial or an event but must eventually settle in a place of trust. If God can use the cross to bring about good, He can certainly use injustice and suffering to bring about His purposes in us as well.

ACTION

Because of God's sovereignty, we can pray, but we must also act.

I regret how many times in my life I've asked God to act and then remained stagnant in my behaviors. There are times when we pray and then manipulate our circumstances in an attempt to answer our prayers. There are also times we are instructed to obey.

If we've prayed, God desires to give us the power to act. God didn't set up creation with Adam and Eve sitting in lawn chairs praying things would happen. They were called to cultivate the soil and tend His creation.

Let's examine this from Paul's perspective. Phillip Yancey brought these texts to my attention in his excellent book on prayer.

"Work hard to show the results of your salvation, obeying God with deep reverence and fear. For God is working in you, giving you the desire and the power to do what pleases Him." –Philippians 2:12b–13

"For I have worked harder than any of the other apostles; yet it was not I but God who was working through me by His grace." –1 Corinthians 15:10b

"My old self has been crucified with Christ. It is no longer I who live, but Christ lives in me." –Galatians 2:20

"For we are God's masterpiece. He has created us

anew in Christ Jesus, so we can do the good things He planned for us long ago." –Ephesians 2:10

Yancey continues, "The partnership binds so tight that it becomes hard to distinguish who is doing what, God or the human partner. God has come that close." (Yancey, Philip 2006)

This means we need …

PRAYER

We must remain in Him. God is moved as we live in relationship with Him. He provides the power to carry out His work. We should ask; we should wrestle; we can argue; we can bring Him our doubts and even our anger. We won't be the first, and, in the process, He will reveal His heart to us. Don't allow a misconception of God's eternal plan to get in the way of what He hopes to accomplish in our lives today. Keep praying, and don't give up.

5.

WRESTLING WITH GOD
IS IT OK TO STRUGGLE WITH GOD?

So be truly glad. There is wonderful joy ahead, even though you must endure many trials for a little while. These trials will show that your faith is genuine. It is being tested as fire tests and purifies gold—though your faith is far more precious than mere gold. So when your faith remains strong through many trials, it will bring you much praise and glory and honor on the day when Jesus Christ is revealed to the whole world.
—I Peter 1:6–7

The year was 1997. At the time, I didn't have my retreating hairline. I had long golden locks strategically parted, flowing slightly past my ears. I may have been growing my first few facial hairs to see if I could pull off a goatee, and I had met a girl.

When I dated someone, I put all my heart and soul into the relationship. I lost friends. I managed to find time I didn't have simply to spend a few more moments with the object of my affection. I never eased into dating. I put a great deal of pressure on my romantic life, often traveling from 0 to serious in 2.5 dates.

I had a firm belief that God didn't want me to waste my time on a girl who wasn't "The One," so I dove in head first in hopes of quickly discerning whether or not my epic quest to find my one true love had finally found its conclusion.

In this instance, I had been dating a nice girl for a couple of months, and it happened again.

After escorting her back to her room and exiting her dormitory, I began to feel something was off. I felt a feeling in my gut or soul similar to a sense of guilt or conviction. Though not audible, it seemed to scream, "She's not 'The One.'" To be honest, and to this day, I'm still uncertain if this was the Spirit of God or the direct result of Mexican Night at the college cafeteria. But, at the time, I felt it was from the Lord.

I left her dorm room, infuriated with God. So, we took a walk on a rural country road. I loudly voiced my frustrations. I screamed at the top of my lungs. I remember the words, "What do You want from me?" venomously coming out of my mouth. I don't remember if my language was churchy. Odds are, it wasn't. I was hurt, and I let God have it.

Somewhere in the midst of my struggle, after running out of tears, I felt the Spirit of God gently bring me peace. I suddenly didn't need to have it all figured out at that moment. Today's grace was enough for today. It was a starry night, and the vastness of the sky slowly gave me comfort regarding God's plans for my life. I walked the last mile in calm and serenity.

Unfortunately, I failed to consider the ability of sound to travel over open plains, so the last portion of my peaceful walk was shared with a local law enforcement officer who had been called out in response to the suicidal college student screaming at the sky.

Those who mature in their prayer lives grow to understand an important truth. Prayer is not about coming to God like we think He wants us to come but approaching Him as we are, and at times this will involve wrestling with His heart and character regarding our circumstances, thoughts and feelings.

One man's wrestling need not mimic another. Some people have calmer dispositions. Being pulled over by a police officer to examine one's mental state is not a litmus test for proper wrestling.

Yet, in the life of every growing disciple, our struggle with God plays a vital role in our character development.

Unfortunately, this type of wrestling has grown out of vogue in much of the church today.

If a Christ-follower develops deep hurts or struggles, our advice is often to pull it together. Everyone has problems. For the sake of the peace in the community, it becomes simpler to farm out our deep hurts to an offsite counselor or by taking a pill (I'm not anti-pill or anti-counselor).

This discomfort gives the impression that the church wants only the profitable parts of their congregation members. We don't want deep questions, severe struggles, or lingering doubts. It's easier to encourage deep wrestlers to simply place their trust in God and get back to doing the necessary tasks vital to keeping the greater operation afloat. It's simpler to admonish the one struggling to focus on exhibiting consistent moral behavior outside the church doors with the hope that any issue will eventually subside.

This posture negates an important Biblical truth.

THERE IS A HISTORY OF WRESTLING IN THE SCRIPTURES

There is a history of complaining and grappling with God among our most spiritually mature forefathers.

Jacob literally had a wrestling match with God. Through the process, he learned more about himself and God. He grew in humility and was changed, not simply emotionally and spiritually, but was even given a physical reminder of his encounter.

Abraham pled and negotiated with God over Sodom and Gomorrah and later with his wife's infertility.

Moses argued with a fiery bush and later on behalf of an obstinate people bent on rebellion.

Most of the book of Job is comprised of chapter after chapter of an oppressed man wrestling with and questioning God.

When reading the Psalms, David had no problem bringing any and every human emotion to the Lord. His recorded struggles later comprised a portion of Israel's hymnal.

I grew up with upbeat hymns and worship. Imagine, after a rough week at work with a corrupt coworker, going to church the following weekend and instead of a peppy song about God's goodness, the worship team does a modern take on Psalm 35:

> Bring shame and disgrace on those trying to kill me; turn them back and humiliate those who want to harm me.
> Blow them away like chaff in the wind—
> a wind sent by the angel of the Lord.

> Make their path dark and slippery,
> with the angel of the Lord pursuing them.
> I did them no wrong, but they laid a trap for me.
> I did them no wrong, but they dug a pit to catch me.
> So let sudden ruin come upon them!
> Let them be caught in the trap they set for me!
> Let them be destroyed in the pit they dug for me. —Psalm 35:4–8

This is a man after God's own heart, and if we read further, these aren't the worst of the songs we refer to as the Imprecatory Psalms. They might be a shock to the system but also a potential comfort to those experiencing injustice.

After experiencing one of the most incredible displays of God's power in Israel's history, Elijah ran away and hid, begging God to end His life.

Old Testament prophets often included in their writings the phrase: "How long, Lord?" They were wrestling in the tension of God's mercy and His justice.

I would even argue that there will still be people wrestling with the Lord in death.

> When the lamb broke the fifth seal, I saw under the altar the souls of all who had been martyred for the word of God and for being faithful in their testimony. They shouted to the Lord and said, "O sovereign Lord, holy and true, how long before you judge the

people who belong to this world and avenge our blood for what they have done to us?"

Then a white robe was given to each of them. And they were told to rest a little longer until the full number of their brothers and sisters – their fellow servants of Jesus who were to be martyred – had joined them. –Revelation 6:9–11

Last time I checked, 100 percent of those who have been martyred are dead. Yet even in death, they are wrestling with God's plan and timing.

Wrestling and even complaining seem to be encouraged in scripture.

J.I. Packer says, "In the Bible, when bad things happen to good people … they complain with great freedom and at considerable length to their God. And scripture does not seem to regard these complaining prayers as anything other than wisdom." (Packer, James I.; Nystrom, Carolyn 2006)

This may seem counter even to scripture itself. Philippians has a famous text often used to control the mouths of children regarding household chores. Chapter 2 of Paul's book says simply, "Do everything without complaining or arguing." –Philippians 2:14

As a community of faith, we are encouraged to abstain from complaining or arguing with or about one another. Still, the pattern of scripture seems to point in the opposite direction regarding our relationship with God. The more we complain to Him, the more at peace we are with those we encounter in the world.

Honesty with God regarding the condition of our souls is a sign of maturity, not immaturity.

PRAYER PROVIDES A PLACE TO WRESTLE

Prayer is a great place to pour out what's inside of us, even if we don't like what we find.

We did nothing to earn our salvation. God loved us while we were still unlovable and self-centered. Yet often, after discovering this love, it is common practice among believers to then feel the need to come to the Father with some semblance of togetherness before approaching Him in prayer.

These thoughts may stem from our understanding of the Levitical priesthood. In those days approaching God was filled with complications. Curtains, procedures and purifications were necessary to approach the Holy of Holies. To misunderstand the holiness of God could have dire consequences. One wrong step by a high priest and the rope tied around their leg might be used to pull their dead body out of the temple. We then mistakenly superimpose their reality onto our own. We assume we must sanctify and purify ourselves before we can approach God.

When Jesus died, the curtain was torn. We can never become holy enough, so God became holiness for us. We can now come to Him as our Abba Father, as our Daddy God. When we approach His throne trying to manufacture our perfection, we insult the perfection God won for us through the work of Christ. We devalue the cross. His work means we can now come to Him with any emotion and struggle we experience.

Psalm 137 is uncomfortable. Many wish it weren't included in scripture, not knowing how to justify its inclusion due to its incongruity with other texts in the Bible.

> O Lord, remember what the Edomites did on the day the armies of Babylon captured Jerusalem. 'Destroy it!,' they yelled. 'Level it to the ground!' O Babylon, you will be destroyed. Happy is the one who pays you back for what you have done to us. Happy is the one who takes your babies and smashes them against the rocks! –Psalm 137:7–9

One might assume this song might not make the cut for the Jewish hymnal due to content or was only performed with the electric harp and distortion pedals. Is this type of wrestling permissible? Was the prayer answered? How does this look like Jesus? It doesn't.

I believe these words represent the Psalmist sharing the actual condition of his heart. God, in other texts, encouraged the Israelites to live in Babylon and pray for its prosperity. This doesn't strike me as the type of prayer God had in mind.

After losing their homes, the Israelites still carried wounds and hurts. Their minds still had fresh images of death and destruction caused by the Babylonians. War rarely brings with it humility. In the case of the Psalmist, vengeance and revenge filled his heart. This wrestling unapologetically made the cut to be included in the holy scriptures. God was not afraid of allowing even this text into His Bible.

Let's connect these thoughts to a more modern example. Imagine a woman employed at a company with a difficult boss. He was promoted to a higher position than her because he dishonestly climbed the corporate ladder by slandering his competition, occasionally fudging the numbers and spreading well-placed gossip to keep any competition at bay. In addition to these issues, the boss is hostile toward this poor woman's faith.

When allowing her mind to wander, she envisions justice and how it might be doled out against this pompous, arrogant supervisor. She daydreams about a moment involving a box filled with picture frames and prized possessions being toted out to a car the man can no longer afford or, even better, an incident involving uniformed men and handcuffs.

Throughout her time under this man's authority, she's handled the situation better than most. When coworkers complained, she remained silent or let other Christian coworkers know she's been praying for him. But inside, she would love to see God work to right this wrong.

She does pray, but when he comes to mind, she finds it hard to develop good thoughts about the man as she speaks to God on his behalf. She knows God has called her to love her enemy, so she suppresses her anger and hatred when speaking to her heavenly Father. Instead, she says general blessings on the man's life, praying what she thinks God wants to hear, as opposed to her true feelings toward her oppressor.

It might be healthier for our fictitious woman to pray, "God, I want him fired, and if you could make it humiliating in the process, it would be all the better. It's what he deserves. Wipe the smug look off his face and give him what he has coming."

Over time, this type of honesty will often springboard

the believer to a place of proper perspective and eventually even sincere love for our enemies. Masking hate doesn't produce love.

Even our blatant sinful thoughts provide a starting place for transformation. If we fail to acknowledge what we are genuinely thinking regarding an enemy, we fail to provide the authenticity necessary for God to begin the process of forming within us His heart and character toward the person.

We should cling to the truth. Truth should always trump and shape our emotions. We are still called to love our enemies with our behaviors, but over time, the discrepancy should dissipate between what we really think about the person during the day and how we approach God about them when we pray. God doesn't want our kind but insincere words. He wants His child coming to Him as they are, no matter what we're filled with.

This is a great thought by Beth Moore:

> The Holy Spirit, who inspired the blessed invitation of the psalmist, did not qualify it with the words, 'Pour out your heart to God if what's inside is nice and sweet.' The concept of 'pouring out' suggests that some of the contents in our hearts need to go— like hurt, anger, despair, doubt, bitterness, unforgiveness, and confusion. The idea is to pour out the bitter waters that well up in our hearts so that God can pour wellsprings of living, sweet waters back in. (Moore, Beth; Crusade for World, Revival 2005)

Some believers' inability to grow in intimacy with God originates in their unwillingness to pour out their bitter waters to Him.

The church then becomes a chemical treatment plant. Instead of recognizing the bitter waters, we develop a chemical concoction capable of lessening the outward effects of our inner nastiness. Or we assume the sour water will clear up with a pinch of sugar, represented by a few good works. Unfortunately, there is no amount of sweetener capable of improving the taste of sewer water.

God wants us instead to pour out the contents of our souls so He can fill those spaces with pure and living water.

Prayer is not simply meant to be a duty or obligation. It's intended to be a safe outlet where we can receive God's grace alongside His assurance that our sins are covered by the work of Jesus.

There is also an additional benefit.

WE DISCOVER A PLAN BEHIND OUR WRESTLING

Wrestling with God often leaves us with answers to questions we weren't even asking.

"God, reveal to me who she is." Above all other prayers, this was the focus of my youth.

Eventually, my prayer was answered. Yet, in the process, God's answer yielded much more than my wife's name.

I was exposed as a follower who didn't trust God as good. At my core, I believed He was holding out on me. He exposed a potential good gift that had been turned into an idol.

During this pursuit, I trusted my feelings and emotions regarding decisions more than I trusted His Word and the community of believers He placed me in.

True to form, when I met my future wife, I had similar feelings during our courtship. The ominous feelings, either whispering or shouting, "This isn't the one," still occasionally entered my mind. But because of God's work through my prayers, I could, in faith, say, "Listen, feelings, this is a woman who loves God. My family, her family and our friends have no reservations about our relationship, and I find her highly attractive." So regardless of my feelings, I took a step of faith.

There are examples of this truth throughout scripture. We may pray for a particular result and get much more. Phillip Yancey points out...

> Like Peter, we may pray for food and get a lesson on racism; like Paul we may pray for healing and get humility. We may ask for relief from trial and instead get patience to bear them. We may pray for release from prison and instead get strength to redeem the time while there. Asking, seeking and knocking does have an effect on God, as Jesus insists, but it also has a lasting effect on the asker, seeker and knocker. (Yancey, Philip 2006)

When we perceive a struggle with God, He is in the background forming His character inside us. Often, the process we go through in receiving an answer has more benefit than the direct answer to the prayer itself.

When we openly struggle with the Lord, we give Him

an opportunity to work in our lives. 1 John is a book about living in the light. In the first chapter, it says this:

> God is light, and there is no darkness in Him at all. So we are lying if we say we have fellowship with God but go on living in spiritual darkness; we are not practicing the truth. But if we are living in the light, as God is in the light, then we have fellowship with each other, and the blood of Jesus, His Son, cleanses us from all sin. –1 John 1:5–7

One of the greatest hindrances to spiritual growth is keeping the dark parts of who we are outside of God's light.

Or put this way – "Prayer invites me to lower defenses and present the self that no other person fully knows to a God who already knows." (Yancey, Philip 2006)

This leads to a few final questions to wrestle through. Why pray to a God who already knows everything about us? If God knows us better than we know ourselves, why bother re-informing Him of the depressing truths about our spiritual condition? Doesn't He understand our struggles at a deeper level than we ever will?

These seem like reasonable inquiries.

Wrestling with God helps us see what He sees.

God is not simply available to give guidance. He desires to do more than instruct us regarding our next steps in life. He is there to provide us with wisdom, to help us ask the right questions, see His heart, and develop a proper posture toward our circumstances. He wants to help us see His truth in the midst of difficulty. He wants us to know Him intimately.

APPLICATION
WRESTLE

There is no requirement to go through the craziness of my journey. We are all uniquely wired. Some question less and trust more. Emotional instability is not a requirement for spiritual growth.

The key isn't how we wrestle but if we wrestle. Life on a fallen planet is a bully. In a world still filled with the effects of sin and death, circumstances will repeatedly poke at us until we react. The more we fail to respond appropriately, the more aggressive the onslaught becomes.

The pattern for many believers is one of superficial trust. Instead of wrestling through injustice or hurt, we either ignore it or make excuses for it. Others cover the wound with an ointment consisting of one part spiritual platitudes and one part Christian nicety. This balm may smooth over the surface but often pushes hurt and anger deeper into our souls.

We then place a Band-Aid with an "I Know God is in Control" graphic over any visible sore, leaving us with the appearance of being normal (even if, over time, we have failed to believe what the graphic says to be true).

The deep-seated anger then festers and eventually finds its way out, often directed toward those we feel safest around. It may manifest in rage or control. Couching these feelings in a religious context often makes the symptoms worse, not better.

God is not the author or initiator of evil, but everything is now under His control and can be used for our benefit.

When Christ died and rose again, the power of sin and death was broken. They both still limp on. We still have funerals. Tornados and hurricanes still touch the ground. People remain evil and hurt one another.

The ascended Christ doesn't cause or orchestrate evil but now has authority over it. Regardless of their best efforts, nothing can separate us from God's love. Evil committed against us now serves as an opportunity to grow in Christ-likeness. Trials endured, once avoided at all costs, now serve to strengthen our faith. Even death is a shadow of its old self. What once was permanent is now a passage to an even greater life. I'm not calling bad good. Sin and death aren't gone, but in Christ, they are humiliated and subservient to God's work in the believer's life.

This truth does not negate wrestling. It encourages it. We want what is true to be true of us. We should want what is true of God's kingdom to be true in the world we live in.

When there is a gap between the two, it should cause the believer to wrestle in prayer.

In most wrestling matches, the goal is to have the most skill and strength. When wrestling with God, the opposite is true.

Jim Cymbala understands the power of prayer more than most. He reminds us of an astounding truth: "God is attracted to weakness. He can't resist those who humbly and honestly admit how desperately they need Him." (Cymbala, Jim 2001)

When we wrestle with God, coming as we are and clinging to Him, we provide Him the opportunity to transform our lives.

6.

UNANSWERED PRAYERS
WHY IS GOD SAYING NO?

Three different times I begged the Lord to take it away.
–2 Corinthians 12:8

All prayers are heard and answered. The response may not always be yes. It might be yes, no or maybe so. Or yes, no or wait. At least, this is what I was told as a child and later taught as a pastor. Catchy phrases are helpful and valuable when they quickly bring a necessary truth to our minds.

But there can be a fine line between help and hurt. If we're not careful, a memorable phrase may feel trite when wrestling in prayer for a prodigal son or daughter bent on rebellion or a spouse who stubbornly refuses a life of faith.

There will be moments when we witness life slowly slip away from a loved one despite our intentional prayers on their behalf for the opposite result. We believed God was capable. We had faith in God's capacity to heal, but unless He recreates a Lazarus scenario, we're now forced to wait for the final resurrection to see our loved ones again.

Complicating these seasons of life are passages of scripture seemingly pointing to promises regarding our prayers.

"Ask and it will be given to you, seek and you will, find and knock and the door will be open to you." –Matthew 7:7

Then Jesus says:

"Remain in me and I in you and you will bear much fruit." –John 15:5

And two verses later states, "Then ask me for anything and it will be given to you." –John 15:7

Though not an implication of the original context, these verses tend to haunt troubled souls and compel the ones suffering to either question God or themselves.

"What are we doing wrong?"

The Bible is filled with big prayers. Fire from heaven consuming enemy forces, droughts, and plagues all come from a simple request. Later the disciples asked God to perform miracles. In response, lame men walked, and the blind received sight. Angels staged a prison break for apostles in reaction to the people of God praying. Our Lord seems undaunted by bold prayers.

Yet often, our far less spectacular requests either take time or aren't answered at all. It makes one wonder if we shouldn't simply pray for Grandma's healing but also for her ability to run a 5k.

For many honest seekers, if an answer doesn't come immediately or in a reasonable time frame, the result is disillusionment. God's no, silence or patience in our situation may make some wonder why we asked God for anything in the first place.

These are important prayers. At times they are matters of life and death. We're not praying for a new sports car, a bigger house or divine favor when picking Powerball numbers. We're pouring out our hearts on behalf of someone else.

How can we believe God hears and listens to us if He sits aloof in heaven, denying such desperate and heart-felt requests? It's a child with cancer. It's a mother with young children. It's the salvation of a loved one.

Many have walked away from their faith after pouring out their hearts to a God they viewed as caring, only to see the answer they eagerly expected denied or withheld from them. It's essential to have a proper perspective regarding unanswered prayers.

Foundational to these questions is an essential truth from scripture. God is committed to the eternal well-being and happiness of His children.

Luke, in His Gospel, quotes the words of Jesus:

> You fathers—if your children ask for a fish, do you give them a snake instead? Or if they ask for an egg, do you give them a scorpion? Of course not! So if you sinful people know how to give good gifts to your children, how much more will your heavenly Father give the Holy Spirit to those who ask Him? –Luke 11:11–13

The greatest gift ever given is the presence of God inside of us. If we value God above anything else, the losses we experience in this life pale in comparison to what we have gained in Christ.

In Him, even a no will be used for our benefit. God's patience is intended to produce His character inside of us and may result in an answer even better than a simple yes or no.

If our faith is contingent upon a favorable answer to prayer, it may reveal that our hope and security rest in the object of the prayer instead of the one we approach in prayer.

In these instances, God may use a tragedy to expose our hearts and bring us back to Himself.

Human behaviors and actions can hinder our communication with God, possibly even preventing a prayer from being answered. We'll work through seven of them in a moment, but before we continue, I want to point out a caveat to this discussion.

WE HAVE NO IDEA WHY SOME PRAYERS GO UNANSWERED

In the Lord's Prayer, we are invited to live in this tension.

"May your Kingdom come soon. May your will be done on earth, as it is in heaven." –Matthew 6:10

We are instructed to look at the world and see where God's kingdom is not and begin to pray that it be brought under His authority. When we witness an abusive situation, start praying for God's kingdom to come. When reading about children living in trees in Africa, pray, "Your kingdom come."

God desires to hear and answer our prayers, but more important than an affirmative response to every one of our inquiries is that His will be done.

An unanswered prayer may very well mean we're doing something wrong, but it might not. Sometimes we won't know or understand the plans or timing of God. The tangled threads of a tapestry will be turned around to reveal beautiful purposes in the next life, but in this one, we're left with a few knots we may not be able to untangle.

I'm comforted by Tim Keller's words in his book on prayer:

"In short, God will either give us what we ask or give

us what we would have asked if we knew everything He knew."(Keller, Timothy 2014)

REASONS A PRAYER MAY GO UNANSWERED

There are, however, occasions where God's unresponsiveness is connected to our attitudes and behaviors. If we speak to God and discover we never seem to be receiving an answer to any of our prayers or the answer is consistently "no," we may need to examine our mindset regarding our prayers.

If we fail to root out these patterns of thinking or acting, our prayers will eventually become nonexistent or remain impotent. The frustrated disciple will then drift into intentionally vague requests (so we can justify that they have been answered) or small requests (so we can help God along if He doesn't come through) or might quit praying altogether.

Let's consider why our prayers may appear to be falling on deaf ears.

REASON 1 –WE FAIL TO PRAY OR PRAY WITH DISTORTED MOTIVES

Scripture says,
"Yet you don't have what you want because you don't ask God for it. And even when you ask, you don't get it because your motives are all wrong—you want only what will give you pleasure." –James 4:2b–3

Some of us fail to receive anything from the Lord because we don't spend any time in prayer. We need not worry about what we ask for because we don't ask in the first place.

James then points to an additional problem. Some manage to ask but do so with the wrong motives.

God wants to respond, but the answer to our prayers may inadvertently contribute to our spiritual detriment. My kids consistently ask me for time on their devices. If I said yes every time they asked, they would never go outside, lose the ability to interact with others of their same species and eventually resemble characters from the Walking Dead.

When we pray for our circumstances to change (because trials make us uncomfortable), we miss the blessing the trial is intended to produce. Or, if we make requests capable of turning the blessings of God into an idol, we reveal we want the handouts of God without the hand of God. We desire what He can provide but don't want Him. God becomes a means to find our happiness instead of the source of our happiness.

Part of prayer is knowing our Father's heart and desires for us. In Class 101 of Christ's school of prayer, He begins the process by teaching us to ask for the right things. This happens through trial and error and in a relationship with Him.

REASON 2– OUR PRAYERS RESEMBLE WITCHCRAFT

Others distort prayer to the point that it looks more occultic than Biblical. They might pray in the right direction but do so as a pagan prays to an idol. They manipulate the hand of God to do their bidding.

"Lord, You are bound by the name of Jesus and Your

holy word. The scriptures state in John 15:7, 'Then ask me for anything, and it will be given to you .' We now pray in the name of Jesus for _____."
What fills the blank is less relevant to this discussion than the perspective in which the prayer is prayed. Those seeking to manipulate God may use scripture, personal sacrifice, a level of faith, or their morality as the basis of their demands. The Bible, their strength of belief or good works, then become ingredients used in casting spells seeking to bind the God of the universe by His commands to bring about their own will and kingdom.

Approaching God through any means outside of the shed blood of Christ becomes a means to control God. Biblical prayer is meant to advance God's reign in the world and reproduce His character inside of us. We are His children, and He is our Father, not a force to manipulate.

REASON 3– WE LOVE OUR SIN MORE THAN WE LOVE GOD

Peter penned a familiar text in the third chapter of His first book, often used at marriage retreats, but the ending points toward a root cause of some unanswered prayers.

> In the same way, you husbands must give honor to your wives. Treat your wife with understanding as you live together. She may be weaker than you are, but she is your equal partner in God's gift of new life. Treat her as you should so your prayers will not be hindered. –1 Peter 3:7

In addressing husbands, Peter is connecting a man's tendency to act like a jerk toward his wife with the effectiveness of his prayer life. A man can't maintain a pattern of yelling and screaming at his spouse and then lift his countenance toward heaven and solemnly pray, "Majestic Father, holy omnipotent great God..." and expect to be heard or for his prayers to be unhindered.

God is pleased to hear a man confess with contrition what a jerk he's been, but harboring unconfessed sin in our lives will hurt our prayers. If they continue at all, they will devolve into a religious discipline of "saying our prayers" instead of genuine engagement with the Father.

Perfection is not a requirement for intercession, but intimacy is difficult when we remain obstinate. This is true in human relationships and our relationship with God. If we desire our sin more than we love God, acknowledgment and confession are good places to find healing. A mistress in marriage or an idol in a relationship with God will each bring devastating consequences to closeness and communication.

REASON 4– WE PRAY IN OUR OWN NAME

We are told to pray in the name of Jesus. My habit is to end every prayer in the name of Jesus. "And we pray all of this in Jesus's name, Amen." More feisty preachers may add a syllable for effect, turning our Savior's name into a three-syllable word. "We ask for this to happen in the name of Ju-EEZ-us."

Many use the name of Jesus as a stamp on their thoughts and communication with God regarding what they believe should happen in our world. Others pray in the name of Jesus instead of praying to other gods or deities worshipped in our world.

To pray in the name of Jesus means approaching God based on what His son has accomplished. Any authority we carry in prayer is connected to His authority. Yet, some pray in the name of Jesus while functionally praying in their own name.

A name carries with it a reputation. A good reputation may grant influence in various arenas of life. A successful business owner may carry weight with city councils or local government. The larger a person's net worth, the greater the influence they may wield in our world. At the first hint of an Amazon corporate expansion, local governments spring into action putting together plans and incentives to lure the corporate giant into their community.

Others who contribute significant amounts of money to political campaigns expect their name to be considered and their causes to be reflected in policy decisions.

To cross a person with influence may mean the loss of a politician's authority and position.

I've never donated to a political campaign. I have opinions on how a follower of Christ should engage in politics. There are causes I'm passionate about. Imagine a scenario where I managed to get a hearing from my national representative. In our conversation, I laid out my desires and hopes for our great nation. She listened politely. I left and returned home. To my shock, when I turned on the local news, this politician continued to vote in ways contrary to how I had instructed her.

I quickly dialed her office and left a message reminding her of who I was and what I said. Does she not know who I am? There are people in this world capable of pulling this woman from her daughter's recital to have a brief conversation. My name is incapable of doing this.

If this is true among men, how much more so should a feeble and fallen human being sense their insignificance and inadequacy when approaching the God of the universe based on their own reputation, wealth or achievements?

Yet many Christians still functionally pray with their worthiness in mind. We approach the throne of grace with our works. We connect our moral behavior and righteousness to receiving what we ask for in prayer. The presence of great works (church attendance, social service, spiritual disciplines and being a better person than most) or the absence of bad ones (abstaining from excessive amounts of alcohol, the lack of a mistress, or a vocabulary devoid of expletives) inflates the ego to the point of entitlement.

The result is far more comical (or, more accurately, tragic) than an average Joe like me seeking influence over a human politician.

When we pray in the name of Jesus, we humbly understand where our access to the Father originates. We come to God through what Christ has done. We then don't come demanding but humbly as we boldly intercede on behalf of ourselves and others.

REASON 5– WE FAIL TO ASK AND KEEP ON ASKING

I grew up with the NIV, and Matthew 7 says, "Ask and you will receive, seek and you will find," (Matthew 7:7) but in this instance, the NLT is more accurate.

"Keep on asking, and you will receive what you ask for. Keep on seeking, and you will find. Keep on knocking, and the door will be opened to you. For everyone who asks, receives. Everyone who seeks, finds, and to everyone who knocks, the door will be opened." –Matthew 7:7–8

It's important to remember that this text comes immediately after Jesus details what it means to live under God's kingdom authority in the Sermon on the Mount. These teachings are filled with seemingly impossible requirements. Love your enemy. Abstain from lustful thoughts. We discover that calling another man a fool is akin to murder in the kingdom of God.

In this context, the command to ask and keep on asking is tied to the righteous life of Christ, not a second home or more favorable circumstances. Consequently, achieving inner goodness isn't the result of a "try hard" mentality. The character of Christ is instead given when we seek and keep on seeking it. We ask for His power to act in obedience while waiting for our inner dispositions to gradually align with Christ's words.

We can ask for anything in this world with no guarantee that we will receive it. There are no promises in scripture regarding the removal of a tumor, extended life for a loved one or a much-desired promotion. Our tenacity in asking, seeking and knocking may or may not be rewarded with our desired result. This shouldn't prevent our asking in any of these scenarios, but these promises are connected to the righteousness of Christ worked out in us.

The promise of God in each of these texts is regarding the inner character of Christ. By His word, we are guaranteed to ripen into who we were originally intended to be, as described by Jesus's words to His followers. Ripening takes time. Lust isn't often eradicated in one prayer but will lessen over time as we seek His power.

Patience doesn't come in a single moment. Gentleness isn't a one-time event where the Holy Spirit descends upon His servant and declares a woman gentle. Love for our enemies isn't the result of an occasional knock on heaven's door. It is, instead, the byproduct of consistent fellowship with the One who, when squeezed, poured out forgiveness toward His oppressors. Fruit doesn't appear in an instant but ripens in season.

As we spend time with God, asking for what He wants to give us, we will begin to receive it. The process happens over the course of a lifetime of prayer.

Some prayers we presume remain unanswered are simply God's gentle "no." When it comes to the righteous character of Christ, the answer will always be "yes." God desires to give it to us, but we must keep asking for it.'

REASON 6– WE PRAY AND NEVER ACT

"I've been praying for my friend for 62 years, and he's yet to come to the Lord."

"Have you ever had a conversation with him over matters of faith?" "No, but I've been faithful in prayer."

Sometimes we pray and forget that while Christ is the Head, we are His hands and feet. They are the only hands and feet He has on this planet.

We tell ourselves we trust God to do His will but often fail to explore how we might play a part in His plan for the one we're interceding for.

We pray for a young couple's marriage but never think of having them over. We pray for the unsaved but never share the Gospel. We ask God to do what He has clearly made our responsibility.

What if God is not simply calling us to pray, but through our prayers, He is empowering and equipping us to act? If we act without praying, we become like Moses killing the Egyptian. We try to accomplish God's purpose without God's power. When we marry our prayers to our actions and obedience, we provide fertile ground for kingdom advancement.

REASON 7– WE ARE ENGAGED IN SPIRITUAL WARFARE

> Then he said, don't be afraid, Daniel. Since the first day you began to pray for understanding and to humble yourself before your God, your request has been heard in heaven. I have come in answer to your prayer. But for twenty-one days the spirit prince of the kingdom of Persia blocked my way. Then Michael, one of the archangels, came to help me, and I left him there with the spirit prince of the kingdom of Persia. Now I am here to explain what will happen to your people in the future, for this vision concerns a time yet to come. –Daniel 10:12–14

When Daniel prays in this text, it appears an angel was dispatched immediately but is held up in a spiritual skirmish.

At the end of his letter to the Ephesians, Paul reminds his friends of a battle outside of our flesh-and-blood existence. He points to a war occurring in the unseen world for the hearts and souls of men.

Spiritual warfare is often either overemphasized or underemphasized in the church. We either encourage the casting out of demons preventing long lines at Home Depot or dismiss the effects of the occultic as purely psychological.

The scriptures address spiritual warfare without making it a central thrust of the epistles or Christ's teaching. There is no appendix in the Bible after the glossary and maps detailing the history of cosmic warfare between heavenly beings. One would assume part of the reason for this omission rests in humanity's innate ability to be distracted from the main thrust of a story by speculating on peripheral drama. To give us more detail might complicate how we assume we are called to fight. Paul encourages us to fight by putting on the righteousness of Christ as armor.

Our power comes from knowing God. He would rather know us intimately than assist us in growing proficient in our ability to exorcise a demon. Sometimes, direct engagement in spiritual warfare is necessary, but our effectiveness is connected more to an intimate relationship with God than proper technique.

God may appear slow in answering our prayers. His slowness may be tied to our dullness, His greater glory, or a battle in the unseen world we aren't privy to.

APPLICATION

TRUST IN THE CHARACTER OF GOD AS REVEALED IN HIS SON JESUS

When struggling with unanswered or ongoing prayers, our focus should remain on Jesus. All we need to know about God's posture toward us is found on the cross.

He gave us His Spirit to live inside of us to remind us of His love.

God will sometimes say no, but His negative response will reap a positive benefit. Even Christ asked His Father to take the cup of wrath away from Him. His prayer was answered with a "no." While we deserve our prayers to go unanswered, He did not. Yet, in Christ, the one person deserving of a divine "yes" was given a "no" so we could be adopted as God's children.

Our faith should be in the Father's love as we pray.

BRIDGE
LISTENING TO GOD

And so we must learn to pray. The child learns to speak because his father speaks to him. He learns the speech of his father. So we learn to speak to God because God has spoken to us and speaks to us. By means of the speech of the Father in heaven His children learn to speak with Him. Repeating God's own words after Him, we begin to pray to Him. We ought to speak to God and He wants to hear us, not in the false and confused speech of our heart, but in the clear and pure speech which God has spoken to us in Jesus Christ. –Dietrich Bonhoeffer

7.

LISTENING TO GOD
GOD'S WORD AS A TOOL FOR COMMUNICATION

Spiritual growth is connected to the Bible. Immediately following our new birth, we are often encouraged to pray, read the Bible and attend church. This is good advice.

We're working through prayer in this book. The church carries its complications, but so does the Bible. How we read our Bibles matters. As a pastor, I don't want my congregation reading the book of Judges using the Israelites as a template for moral guidance or Jacob's family as a pattern for healthy family dynamics. I don't want a seeker mistaking the Old Testament Law as an attainable avenue for making oneself acceptable to God.

The Bible communicates God's character through an overarching narrative of His faithfulness. Through the story, God maintains both His love and His justice. The two meet in their fullest form on the cross, where the Son's sacrifice fulfills the wrath of God toward sin while demonstrating the full extent of the Father's love.

The Bible is a redemption story but is additionally described as living and active in the book of Hebrews. It remains a valuable tool for cultivating vibrant growth in the lives of maturing believers.

For a great deal of my life, I viewed prayer and scripture reading as two essential but separate disciplines. I would read my Bible devotionally, study or even meditate on its words. After closing it, I would then struggle in prayer, bemoaning my inability to hear from God.

As we transition from practical wrestling to a Christ-given model, an important resource is found in the scriptures. The Bible is the most common form of communication a Christ-follower has with the Father. When we pray with our Bibles open, we allow God to speak directly to us. He invites us to respond to the words on the pages relationally. Scripture doesn't eliminate a wandering mind, but it certainly helps.

When I struggle to praise God, instead of feeling the burden of fresh content daily, I open the Psalms. Throughout the hymnal, I find myself connected to others wrestling with God in ways I might not be. At other times, I discover comfort in a shared human experience. Often, I find it helpful to view the Psalmist's work through a Christological perspective, praising God for a more complete understanding given in Christ. Allowing the Psalms to assist us in worship is a great help in prayer.

The words of Jesus lay an important foundation regarding the nature of His kingdom. Teachings in the epistles point toward the healthy implications of the Gospel in our daily lives and Christian community. Rather than praying His kingdom come with directives we assume are in line with His desires, we find power in praying His words knowing scripture will always be in line with His will.

The Sermon on the Mount brings to light the discrepancy between our inner thought lives and outward behaviors. The text serves to expose sins in need of confession to one who desires to forgive them.

By keeping the scriptures open as we pray, we

provide opportunities for God to speak first and direct our conversations. This isn't a new habit in Christian history.

George Müller was a man of prayer. He was also known as a man of great compassion, having created a massive network of orphanages in England during the 1800s. He would periodically sit a group of orphans down for a meal without food within the home and ask for God's provision. As they waited, inevitably, through various circumstances, the Lord would provide.

In George Müller's prayer life, he underwent a significant shift in how he approached God in prayer. He says this about the change:

> The difference, then, between my former practice and my present one is this: formerly, when I rose, I began to pray as soon as possible, and generally spent all my time till breakfast in prayer, or almost all the time. At all events I almost invariably began with prayer... But what was the result? I often spent a quarter of an hour, or half an hour, or even an hour on my knees before being conscious to myself of having derived comfort, encouragement, humbling of soul, etc.; and often, after having suffered much from wandering of mind for the first ten minutes, or quarter of an hour, or even half an hour, I only then really began to pray.
>
> I scarcely ever suffer now in this way. For my heart being nourished by the truth, being brought into experimental [today we would say "experiential"] fellowship with

God, I speak to my Father and to my Friend (vile though I am, and unworthy of it) about the things that He has brought before me in His precious Word. It often now astonishes me that I did not sooner see this point. (Whitney, Donald S. 2015)

It's vital to be grounded in the Word of God for many reasons, but it is especially important in our prayer lives.

REASONS TO INCLUDE SCRIPTURE IN OUR COMMUNICATION WITH GOD

REASON 1– WE SEE GOD FOR WHO HE IS AND WHO HE IS REVEALED TO BE

Humanity has been praying to various gods for most of history. Prayer has little power if it's simply directed toward the universe.

Most of us are bent toward creating a god of our choosing. We go to our preferred worship center or Christian bookstore to the Build-a-God workshop and simply pick out the attributes we like.

Eugene Peterson makes this point:

Left to ourselves we will pray to some god who speaks what we like hearing, or to the part of God we manage to understand. But what is critical is that we speak to the God who speaks to us, and listen to everything He speaks to us. There is a difference between praying to an unknown god whom we hope to discover in our praying, and praying to a known God, revealed through Israel and Jesus Christ, who speaks our language. In the first, we indulge our appetite for religious fulfillment; in the second we practice obedient faith. The first is more fun, the second is a lot more important. What is essential in prayer is not that we learn to express ourselves, but that we learn to answer God. (Peterson, Eugene H. 1991)

When we pray, we interact and communicate with a revealed God in scripture. We are answering a God who has chosen to disclose Himself in the person of Jesus Christ.

This helps alleviate the feeling of talking to air. By rooting ourselves in scripture, we pray to a specific person who can be known.

When we read the Bible, we see all manner of dysfunction. God is not silent regarding human depravity. Even our heroes of the faith fell short. As we examine their stories, we can see their vice in ourselves, but more importantly, we witness how God relates to the weakness of humankind.

Apart from reading the Bible, we miss who God has shown Himself to be. By praying with God's Word open, we can know and relate to the one we're praying to.

REASON 2– WE SEE THE DISCREPANCY BETWEEN OUR LIVES AND GOD'S PERFECTION

One of the most comforting texts in all of scripture is found in Colossians chapter 1.

It says there…

"Yet now He has reconciled you to Himself through the death of Christ in His physical body. As a result, He has brought you into His own presence, and you are holy and blameless as you stand before Him without a single fault." –Colossians 1:22

I think I'm as encouraged by verse 23 as I am with 22…

"But you must continue to believe this truth and stand firmly in it. Don't drift away from the assurance you received when you heard the Good News." –Colossians 1:23a

Our lives are a mixed bag of the beliefs we know to be true of ourselves in Christ and the tug in our flesh pulling us away from our God-given identity. We drift away from who God says we are. Because of this tension, we must be consistently reminded of our new identity. It becomes necessary to have the Gospel preached to us daily.

When we drift, we begin to believe the lies of the world. Praying through scripture points us toward truth and helps us stand fast in who we are in Christ.

In Him, we are perfect. In our actions and motivations, we remain works in progress.

We have bodies still desirous of control.

The Bible helps us see these controlling interests and provides space for God to begin working on them.

The Bible isn't intended to condemn a Christ follower, but gently or, at times, not so gently reveal work still needing to be done. We may then, in faith, confess and ask Him to work out His character inside of us. The flesh begins to lessen in its influence. This process isn't instantaneous but happens over time.

REASON 3– WE SEE TRUTH TO COMBAT DECEPTION

> For you are the children of your father the devil, and you love to do the evil things he does. He was a murderer from the beginning. He has always hated the truth because there is no truth in him. When he lies, it is consistent with his character; for he is a liar and the father of lies. –John 8:44

Scripture rarely commands us to change the way we feel. When it does, the process of changing how we feel is connected to the way we think. In Romans 12, spiritual transformation is connected to a renewal of the mind (Romans 12:2), not our emotional well-being. In Philippians, Paul encourages the reader to "fix their thoughts," (Philippians 4:8) not get a handle on how they feel. James ties joy amid trial to a consideration of what the trials may accomplish in the believer's life. (James 1:2)

It is easy to allow our emotions to dictate our actions. Our default is allowing how we feel to determine what we do. What we foster internally will eventually manifest itself externally. Often our emotions dictate how we're doing spiritually.

The cause of a great deal of emotional trauma is a belief in a lie. We tell ourselves we aren't good enough, that others wouldn't love us if they knew the dark spots in our souls, or that we must perform if we want to experience God's love in our lives.

The devil is a deceiver. He is the father of lies and a liar. His words will always work to push us in one of two directions. He will whisper shaming lies or prideful lies. On one end of the spectrum, he seeks to convince us of our unworthiness. He points out big sins Jesus could never cover, or he might accuse us of not working hard enough. On the other end, he whispers pride-producing lies. Each of these is designed to bloat our egos and push us away from dependence to independence.

Jesus responded in the desert with scripture. When confronted with temptation, His mind was fixed on truth. He felt hungry. He felt like avoiding the cross. His emotions, however, failed to dictate His actions because His thoughts were firmly fixed on the words of God.

Beth Moore says this:

> As long as our minds rehearse the strength of our stronghold more than the strength of our God, we will be impotent. As we pray the Word of God, acknowledging His limitless strength and transcendent dominion, the truth will begin to eclipse the lies. We will realize that in our weakness He is strong and that as we bend the knee to His lordship, God is more than able to deliver us. (Moore, Beth; Crusade for World, Revival 2005)

This victory is impossible if we don't open the scriptures allowing ourselves to be consistently exposed to God's truth.

APPLICATION

WE SHOULD OPEN THE LINES OF COMMUNICATION BETWEEN OURSELVES AND GOD BY OPENING HIS WORD

God communicates through the Bible. He certainly speaks in other ways as well. He uses creation, His people, and occasionally our circumstances to impart wisdom, give direction and answer questions. But each must be measured against the Word of God.

His Word is also not limited to one venue. He speaks privately with each of His children, corporately as its text is worked through on a Sunday morning. God communicates through His Word in small and large groups, coffee shops, and workplaces.

God desires to speak into our circumstances. This can happen by praying through scripture or simply reading the text with a mind toward obedience. The whole of God's Word is intended to speak into our lives.

If we want to know general principles for making life work, allowing us to live good lives, treating people well, and, when applied, often leads to prosperity, read the book of Proverbs.

If we then want to know what to do when we do everything the Proverbs say and still face tremendous suffering and unexplainable pain, look to the book of Job.

If we need permission to struggle and cry out to God, look to the Psalms.

Even the genealogies and the hard-to-read books of the Bible serve as reminders of a continuous story rooted in human history. The stories aren't fables, and their trail eventually helps to connect Christ to both Abraham and Adam.

In the New Testament, the Epistles help us see what growth should look like as we mature in our relationships with God.

When God seems distant, when the Father's face seems hidden, one need only flip the Bible open to the Gospels and look at the person of Jesus Christ.

To open the pages of scripture is to present God with an opportunity to speak to His child. In-depth study, broad overview reading, meditation, and memorization each provide God a chance to speak.

When we struggle with what to say to God, it may be a good habit to listen to what He has spoken to us first. In filling our prayer times with God's Word, we may find our typical monologue begins to change into a dialogue.

A BRIEF WORD ON FASTING

When I was younger, I nearly quit the discipline of fasting. Before I continue, let me first set the record straight. I've never been a "forty days in the wilderness without a cheeseburger" type of a faster. I'm more of a "skip breakfast and lunch then grab two half-price doughnuts on the way home from work to consume before the evening meal" type of a faster. I know the rules regarding fasting. I'm not supposed to look like I'm skipping a meal and shouldn't tell anyone when I'm doing it. Yet, for half a decade, I struggled to feel the positive effects of fasting. Jesus, when asked about the disciples' failure to fast, didn't discount the practice. He instead postponed the practice until after He left them. I assumed this wasn't only applicable to the original 12 apostles, so I wanted to make it a part of my spiritual disciplines.

My problem was that a practice I assumed would make me more holy seemed to do the opposite. The days I chose to fast were often the days I found myself most irritable. I was distracted, had a short temper and found myself more annoyed with humanity than on the other six days of the week. I'm typically a pleasant human being to be around. Most people think I'm friendly. I would fast and not particularly like the guy I saw in the mirror. Over time I began to realize that instead of being a hindrance, this exposure is an important byproduct of fasting. Most of us live with a veneer of nicety capable of helping us navigate slight grievances, minor relational bumps, and our commute home from work. Fasting dramatically thins this layer and exposes what's underneath the surface.

I thought fasting caused me to be irritable. Fasting exposed me as irritable. Abstaining from food causes toxins to be physically released from our bodies, including ones making our breath smell bad. It seems to have a similar effect spiritually. Soul issues find their way to the surface during fasting. It gives us clarity regarding our present spiritual condition. Fasting can help create content for confession in prayer.

Others fast for spiritual breakthroughs or over major decisions. Jesus's fast came before embarking on His ministry and choosing His disciples. In conjunction with prayer, fasting may, over time, bring clarity regarding a decision. I've served on boards where fasting was the catalyst in moving us past a season we felt stuck. The same can be true of a personal spiritual breakthrough as well. When we fast, we intentionally weaken ourselves. God delights in working through human weakness.

Fasting is the only form of suffering we can willingly choose for ourselves. Human history is full of those who faithfully suffered for their faith. My suffering is often connected to a spotty internet connection or Culver's forgetting to put grilled onions on my butter burger. The value of suffering is great. Peter reminded his readers that those who suffer physically are finished with sin. (1 Peter 4:1) He's not suggesting we never sin, but that suffering shifts our gaze from this life to the next. With this in mind, there have been sects of people who seek to place themselves in scenarios where they might intentionally suffer. Some early followers of Christ would whip themselves, causing bodily harm, to reap the benefits of Peter's words. I don't see anything from early church practice or Jesus's teaching justifying these behaviors. Persecution and suffering are gifts given to purify God's people but aren't meant to be pursued. The one exception to this is fasting. The invitation to fast is especially important in prosperous countries where the opportunity for physical suffering is limited. It might be one of the few ways to enjoy the benefits of suffering without being directly persecuted.

I'm not a doctor, and certainly understand there are nuances and complications surrounding food intake. For those who've battled eating disorders or can't fast for health reasons, many great disciplines are available to help develop spiritual fortitude. Others may find a reduced-calorie diet may be a form of sacrifice.

As we transition from practical wrestling to a Christ-given model of prayer, it's important to remember that both an open Bible and an empty stomach can be invaluable resources in connecting intimately with our Creator.

PART 2
A CHRIST-GIVEN MODEL

INTRO

It's necessary to wrestle through issues surrounding the importance of prayer, God's sovereignty over world events and unanswered prayers. I hope the previous chapters have helped build or rebuild a desire to pray. With this desire, a transition must be made from questions of "why" to a question of "how."

I appreciate the disciples' request. While Jesus walked the earth, it wasn't hard to connect the power of God demonstrated through Jesus and the commitment of the Son to be in the presence of His Father each morning consistently and at times throughout the night.

The disciples saw the habit but didn't understand the "how." In the previous chapter, I mentioned the importance of praying with the pages of the Bible open. This is a helpful practice, but not how Jesus responded to the disciples' inquiry: Lord, teach us to pray.

Jesus's response to their request is one of scripture's more underused and misunderstood texts. I find it remarkable that a text memorized by so many carries such little practical application to most believers' daily prayer lives.

Ironically, the words of the prayer are recited over and over in services without much thought as to how they might be used to instruct a disciple on how to pray. Reciting the Lord's Prayer in corporate prayer may aid in memorization, but the model prayer was never intended to be ritualistically repeated by the disciples with little daily impact. Immediately after presenting what we refer to as the Lord's Prayer, Jesus instructed them to refrain from babbling on in repetition like pagans in hopes of moving the hand of God.

The original audience would have known Jesus was giving them an outline to structure their prayers. The religious leaders had their complex outlines. The disciples were asking Jesus about His.

Most relationships don't exist within a well-defined framework. After a day of work, my wife and I don't pull out our notecards and work through an outline discussing our day. However, on a date, we may pull cards out of a chat pack capable of expanding the scope of our typical topics to know one another better.

Jesus's outline doesn't prohibit spontaneity or rule out times of anguish. We aren't instructed through our tears to progress only through a defined set of bullet points.

Paul often shares his prayers for the readers when writing the churches. Not once does he mention the Lord's Prayer. Even Jesus in the garden fails to cover every point of His own outline when praying to His father regarding the cup of wrath.

To frame our communication with God solely with the Lord's Prayer in mind isn't a faithful application of Jesus's words. Yet when embraced as a typical structure for our prayer lives, this pattern has the power to slowly change our lives, increase our faith and develop intimacy with our Heavenly Father.

8.

OUR FATHER IN HEAVEN
PRAYING TO A DAD WHO CARES

It's not always easy being a dad.

There are perks.

If I don't give the kids the answer they're looking for consistently, they will pass within five feet of me and travel half a block to bug their mother.

In some households, the dad gets the first pick of meat off the grill.

Often there's dad's chair (a recliner everyone in the family knows fits dad's body alone). It's positioned at a premium angle to view the tv and is conducive to a Sunday afternoon nap.

Regardless of the perks, there is a weight inherent in being a dad. God has chosen the image of a father to describe how He relates to us in prayer. It doesn't mean a mom is less critical than a dad, but fatherhood remains God's primary role in relating to His people.

Often our impressions of God are based on the presence or absence of our earthly fathers.

Having a dad who instilled a solid work ethic in their child but never smiled, stopped to play with them, joked, or said, "I love you" will impact how his child relates to God.

This scenario will tempt the child to define their relationship with God by what they do. They may serve faithfully but never pause long enough to allow their heavenly Father to delight in them. They constantly wonder if they've done enough to please God. Even if His love is accepted as doctrinal truth, His affection will remain connected to their performance.

Other fathers may impact their children through their disinterest. A father who entered the front door after work, immediately flipped on the television, logged onto a computer or escaped to the garage will distort a proper understanding of God as Father.

A disinterested father may mistakenly lead the child to believe God is distant and uninterested in us.

Understanding God as a good Father is foundational in learning how to pray. The Lord's Prayer begins with an important phrase: "Our Father, who is in heaven." –Matthew 6:9

It's necessary to approach a superior as they desire to be approached. If Mrs. Smith is our boss, we will address Mrs. Smith as Mrs. Smith until she permits us to call her Katy. After earning multiple degrees, some desire to be referred to as Dr. or professor. I have those in my congregation who are uncomfortable calling me my given name unless it's prefaced by the title "pastor."

If this is true in response to human accolades, how much more so a relationship with God? Yet, the first words of the Lord's Prayer are "Our Father," who is in heaven. He exists beyond us in a place of infinite authority. He is powerful and reigns over the heavens, but He still encourages us to call Him Father in prayer. The fatherhood of God was and is a radical concept for the religious to grasp.

God is otherly. When we speak to God, there is a

level of religious respect we believe is necessary when communicating with a deity. While other gods might require human sacrifice to achieve an audience or temple prostitution to draw their lustful attention, the God of the Bible is different.

In Judaism, the layer upon layer of holiness communicated through the temple structure seemed to point to a God who was untouchable. Conversely, the presence of the temple itself within the community demonstrated God's desire to be near His people.

In the incarnation, God came near, so near the religious leaders failed to understand the gravity of what was happening in their midst. They had grown more interested in pleasing God through their behaviors than knowing Him. Part of their struggle was rooted in how this young rabbi encouraged His followers to approach God in a relationship. In their minds, Jesus was an uneducated and untrained Galilean hillbilly who had no right to teach the people His thoughts on God. In addition to His teaching, they were infuriated by both how He addressed God and encouraged others to do the same.

"Our Father, who art in heaven."

This angered them because it made a conversation with a holy God close and intimate. Didn't Jesus understand that the presence of God was only accessible once a year when a consecrated priest went in to offer sacrifices to God?

With this image in mind, the idea of God desiring a father/son relationship with a human would have seemed incomprehensible, yet this is how Jesus encouraged His followers to pattern their prayers.

Paul later spoke about the nature of our relationship with God when he said to the Romans...

"So you have not received a spirit that makes you fearful slaves. Instead, you received God's Spirit when He adopted you as His own children. Now we call Him, "Abba, Father." For His Spirit joins with our spirit to affirm that we are God's children." –Romans 8:15–16

The Spirit inside of us cries out, "Abba, Father." –Galatians 4:6 The closest translation we have to this word is "Daddy" or "Papa." I would assume the Spirit would cry out words like "your majesty," "kind sir," or "holy omnipotent potentate."

Our flesh wants to approach God with impressive language to wow Him or unconsciously manipulate Him to do what we want Him to do.

We assume a need to prepare ourselves to be in His presence. Clean up, act right, get it together, and then we can approach God. I've prayed with people who feel the necessity to approach God with a King James accent.

The image of Father is the exact opposite. My kids never look at their faces or clothing before talking to me. When they were younger, they'd have snacks plastered all over their face and want to hug me. They had no inhibitions about sitting on me. As they've grown older, my only requirement is pants.

Yet this is the image given to us by Jesus in prayer. We have been adopted into a family and can now approach God our Father with the boldness of a child.

However, this new relationship is not without complications.

ADOPTIONS ARE HARD

"God decided in advance to adopt us into His own family by bringing us to Himself through Jesus Christ. This is what He wanted to do, and it gave Him great pleasure." – Ephesians 1:5

"We, too, wait with eager hope for the day when God will give us our full rights as His adopted children, including the new bodies He has promised us." –Romans 8:23b

Most of us know parents who have adopted either domestically or globally. Others are reading these pages who have themselves been adopted. It's a beautiful act, and there may not be another undertaking one can do on earth more closely resembling what God did for us.

It can also be challenging. There are success stories alongside heartbreaks for those who invited one outside the family in.

Parents who experienced little difficulty raising their biological children, adopt, and unexpectedly experience rejection and rebellion.

Adoption creates a variety of challenges. An adopted child may continue to feel a sense of abandonment. There is often trauma associated with a child's previous life. Moving from one culture to another is often a shock.

The joys of the adoption are wonderful. Our previous father was cruel and ended up being a slave driver. He promised the world and then abandoned us. God saw us in our rejection and offered to adopt us as His sons, but our old father continues to sow seeds of doubt regarding our new Father's acceptance.

Adoptions are also costly. On an earthly level, the legal fees can be astronomical. But with God, it was even more so. He sent His Son so we could be adopted as sons (even the ladies are sons in Christ and guaranteed a full inheritance).

Along with great joy, there may still be lingering questions in the chosen person's mind. Is He listening? Can I trust Him? Is He good?

Our pattern of prayer should begin with a reminder of God's heart toward us. He desires us to approach Him because, as Philip Yancey says…

"Our most treasured gift to God, that which God can never force, is love. Every parent knows it as the one response most valued in their children and the one they are least able to compel." (Yancey, Philip 2006)

There will be adoption pains, but they are not due to the insufficient love of God but are rooted in the distrust of the one adopted. It's a dynamic we must continually work through to develop intimacy with God as Father.

WHY PRAYING TO GOD AS FATHER MATTERS

My wife and I have aims in parenting. We hope to someday exist with our kids living self-sufficient lives outside our homes if possible. Our wish is to instill within them enough personal hygiene that they will attract a spouse and provide us with a grandkid or two. We want our kids to know Jesus and have lives reflective of this knowledge.

As our heavenly Father, God has His desires for His children.

1– GOD DESIRES TO REPRODUCE HIS CHARACTER INSIDE OF US

"This is the great object of a Father in education – to reproduce in His child His own disposition and character." (Murray, Andrew 1885)

We desire this in our children. We want them to lose our dysfunction and carry on our family's greater qualities.

How much more so does God want to form the character of Christ within us? He desires to give freely of His love, patience, kindness, mercy and self-control.

These and more are gifted to us in Christ. They are family traits, but like our kids, they take time to develop.

The more time a son spends with his earthly father, the more the family's mannerisms, postures and speech patterns become present in a boy's life. What often looks forced and unnatural as a small child eventually becomes natural as the boy matures. The same is true when we pray to a Heavenly Father. What at first appears forced will, over time, grow to become more natural.

2 – HE WORKS TO TEACH US HOW TO ASK FOR THE RIGHT THINGS

Kids can ask for dumb things. A young girl living in an urban area might whine and complain about not getting a pony for her birthday. A four-year-old barely able to grasp a toy car might ask for a monster truck for Christmas. As parents, part of our job is to teach our kids how to ask for the right things.

God is trying to do the same with us.

Our greatest desire may be for a second home, a

raise, or a shiny new object. We may pray to be protected from trials, suffering and pain. We may simply be focused on daily needs. When squeezed, the requests we make of God at our subconscious or even conscious level are often misguided.

We ask: "Why are you doing this to me?" Instead of, "What are you hoping to develop in my character through this?" We plead, "Please make my pain go away." If God's answer is no, we need to shift our prayers. "God, will you please show me your power through my pain and give me the strength for today?" Scripture does not forbid our imperfect requests. Our communication with God alone is worth the misguided inquiries. Often our selfish requests allow God to transform what we ask into a request more in line with His will for our lives.

Over time, our requests shift from our comforts to God's glory, and ultimately, these petitions result in our good and development. We begin to receive real patience as opposed to instant gratification. We receive character as opposed to stuff and a life of ease. It's part of what a good parent does.

3– TO SHARE HIMSELF

God created humanity to share in His love. He wants to be in a relationship with us and invites us into a relationship with Him for no other motive than to allow us to share in His love and joy.

Many approach God in prayer, wondering what we must give Him to receive an audience. Jesus's invitation is much different. Our posture should be to approach

God in awe of how much He desires to provide us in a relationship with Him.

I want what many parents want when my children are grown and gone. I pray they are healthy adults who aren't addicted to drugs, only interested in an inheritance, or who appear at holidays bitter over how I've deeply wounded them. Most importantly, I want my kids to know Jesus.

My reasoning behind these hopes is not connected to the ability to brag about my kids over a cup of coffee in my retirement years. When my children embrace the better parts of me, they'll be better for it. I want more than moral behavior. If they did everything I ever asked of them but failed to call or desired to spend time with me, I'd be crushed.

Unfortunately, this scenario plays out in the prayer lives of God's children. Many do what He commands apart from a relationship with Him. Duty is meant to be exchanged for trust. Our faith should be placed in a person, not a process. And this person is a Father who desires to be in a relationship with His children.

APPLICATION

APPROACH GOD WITH CHILD-LIKE

When we begin to pray the Lord's Prayer to help structure our communications with God, we start with our primary relationship with the one to whom we pray. An outline is secondary to a relationship.

By praying "our Father," we are reaffirming our adoption. We take our place as a son in the father/son dynamic. The nature of the relationship allows for incredible flexibility in our prayer lives. We are free to simply spend time in

His presence telling Him about our days, journaling our feelings, or venting frustrations.

It can also be the beginning of a structured prayer time where we work through the various movements of the Lord's Prayer, allowing our sonship to permeate each request.

To miss this dynamic is the equivalent of an eight-year-old dressed in a three-piece suit with a proposal and PowerPoint presentation about the benefits of going to a water park. Most parents would laugh until they realized their child was serious. There would be a tragedy in thinking being put together was a requirement for gaining an audience with a parent.

I love the following quote:

> Jesus likened prayer to a child approaching the father. A child who crawls into her father's lap with a fantasy Christmas list may not get everything she desires. But the very fact that she crawled into his lap, making known her deepest desires, helps cement the bond of love the father cherishes above all else. We do far better to act like a trusting child, presenting foolish requests and letting the Father make judgments than to fret in advance over appropriate petitions. (Yancey, Philip 2006)

Some call Jesus their BFF or might wear the classic "Jesus is my Homeboy" shirt. When we observe these fashion statements, they might and maybe even should rub us the wrong way. Yet, if these someones consistently approach Jesus as they are, even if it's flippant, they provide a place to start. Suppose they continue to spend time with God in daily prayer. In this instance, we may find they are more likely to establish an intimate relationship with Jesus and grasp the holiness of God over time than the person who consistently says their prayers without honestly evaluating their spiritual condition, focusing instead on what they think God wants to hear instead of communicating the desires of their heart.

Our tendency as Christ's followers is to catch ourselves in our selfishness instead of approaching God as we are in the moment. This might explain Jesus's insistence that we come to God like children.

> Nothing exposes our selfishness and spiritual powerlessness like prayer. Little children never get frozen by their selfishness. Like the disciples, they come just as they are, totally self-absorbed. We don't critique our toddlers for walking imperfectly and stumbling. We are excited for their effort. God also cheers when we come to Him with our wobbling, unsteady prayers. (Miller, Paul E. 2017)

The only way we fail at praying is if we quit. The only way we miss out on Christ's character being formed in us is by failing to ask for it. We must keep coming, praying, and even in failure, remain persistent and honest with a Dad who loves us.

9.

MAY YOUR NAME BE KEPT HOLY

WORSHIP IN PRAYER

There are events in life that a good friend will never let you forget.

It was a brilliant idea meant to solve an age-old problem. It can be a chore to get teenagers to engage in worship. My friend and I were jointly planning a mission trip with our combined youth groups and came across a great idea from another youth minister to spice up our times of worship. Instead of simply engaging our kids in singing, we would allow them to assist in making music in an unorthodox and creative manner.

It was a great plan. Pick up random noise-making items from a local thrift shop. Place them in an opaque bag. Toss them onto the floor at the beginning of worship and allow the kids to scramble for their noisemaker of choice. After the chaos, they could shake, grate, or smack their items in worship. It was a great plan.

Unfortunately, my fellow youth pastor Justin and I were on a limited budget, so after being priced out of the market by the local thrift stores, we decided to hit the free tables at a few garage sales. At the first of these sales, I experienced one of the most embarrassing moments of my life.

As we pulled up to our first yard sale, we knew we

had hit the jackpot. There were ice cube trays, containers we could fill with dried beans and various metal objects capable of being smacked together without causing bodily harm. We wouldn't need to go to another sale after we plundered this one.

As we loaded up our plastic bags, I saw it. It was to be my instrument, unique in its build with a sound all its own. It was going to be my chosen noisemaker to bring praise to our Great God on our trip.

I put it in the bag. Then, a few minutes later, I realized Justin had taken it out of the sack and put it back on the table. Indignant, I took it and placed it back in the bag.

As if he was dull to my vision or seeking to rob me of my opportunity to worship the Lord in a new way (or I had begun to wonder if maybe he was a little jealous), a few moments passed, and it was again back on the same table.

I had had enough. If he continued his behavior, the world might be robbed of a new worship movement. It had witnessed David and his harp, Phil Keaggy on the guitar and now me with this.

I began to believe it was time to give him a demonstration in song. So, I picked an easy one. "Lord, I lift Your name on high … Shwiiiisshhhiiii, Shwiiiiiishii. Lord, I love to sing Your praises … Shwiiiishhhiii, Shwishhhiiiii."

A maternal-looking lady behind me began to burst into laughter, but I assumed it was because I was singing at a garage sale.

Before I could turn my one song into a worship set, my good buddy finally looked at me and said, "Travis, that's a breast pump."

Worship is hard. Beyond getting teenagers to engage,

it's also difficult to figure out why we are called to be people of praise.

Hallowed be your name.

Worship isn't only included in the Lord's Prayer; it's where we are encouraged to start. Paul urges Roman believers not to think of themselves more highly than they ought, yet the opposite seems to be true regarding our praise of God. It appears our thoughts are never quite high enough when thinking of the Almighty.

In our flesh, this is awkward. Humanity is rarely drawn to people possessing a need for affirmation. Few of us want to spend time with others who need those around them telling them how wonderful they are.

If we fail to understand how God is different from humanity regarding our praise, it will cripple our worship. Some go through life lip-syncing praises while their heart isn't in it. Others fake a little hand-raising or close their eyes, hoping everyone thinks they're worshipping along with the rest of the group.

Even in energetic worship environments, some may wonder if they are being moved by incredible music or by the presence of God.

Worship wars have been fought since the early days of the church. This makes sense, as our enemy wants nothing more than to prevent those made in God's image from doing what they are created to do. The battles may be identified as hymns versus modern worship, upbeat versus contemplative or disputes over volume level, but often these disagreements reveal something much worse. Worship has become an opportunity to take instead of give.

If this is true of us corporately, it is certainly true of us privately.

Understanding how to worship through our prayers is vital to a vibrant prayer life. If we fail to mature in this discipline, our view of God will remain distorted or small.

The first request in Jesus's model prayer begins with holiness.

The word holy carries with it significant weight. It makes me feel like my prayers should sound or feel like the singing of the Lord's Prayer with a booming voice and much vibrato. In reality, the word is far simpler.

THE WORD HOLY MEANS TO SET SOMETHING APART

We begin by referring to Him as "Our Father who is in heaven." We first acknowledge the closeness of the relationship He desires, but "who is in heaven" speaks to His nature as someone otherly or apart from us.

When I pray, "Holy be your name," it isn't natural. On one extreme, my flesh prefers to worship itself and refuses to acknowledge God as set apart. On the other, I would struggle to pray for a God (who is already clearly holy) to be more holy.

Or I would pray for God's name to be holy "out there." "Lord, in my life be holy, in my church be holy, in the world be holy." To be honest, it felt redundant. Tim Keller summarizes these struggles with a few questions and an important point.

> "Holy be your name. Why should we pray this? Isn't God's name already holy?

We can't make it more so. His name is holy,
but our use of it is not. (Keller, Timothy 2014)

To pray "Holy be your name" both acknowledges God's character while functionally placing Him in the proper place in our lives.

Often what appears sanctimonious isn't at all. Worship often resembles a wrestling match more than eloquent speech.

It may sound like, "Lord, I want to buy this thing. This thing is what's on my mind right now. This thing makes me happy to even think about it. Oh, my soul yearns and even faints for this thing. When my mind wanders, it wanders to this thing. Lord, I pray that You will be above this thing."

For me, it's often an item on Craigslist that I probably don't need. It can also be an event, a job situation, marriage, unemployment, or a nagging sin. The number of things we can fixate on is nearly unlimited.

When we pray, "Holy be your name," we are taking time to place God in the proper place in our lives. It may involve confessing and identifying lesser things currently taking priority over Him. Making God's name holy should lead to worship, but practically, it's a reordering of our loves. If we fail to do this, we will find that the focus of our prayers will end up serving the aforementioned thing over God Himself.

Often our problems in life don't stem from loving terrible desires. Our troubles occur because we love lesser things more than we love the best thing.

Life doesn't work as intended when God is an accessory or a means to getting what we want out of life. This is a drift we all battle. By daily praying, "Holy be your name," we keep the blessings of God from taking the place of God on the throne of our lives. It allows us to fall in line with the created order, which is the next point.

YOU WERE CREATED TO LOVE GOD ABOVE ALL ELSE

A cynic might say, "Neat trick, God of the Universe. Create a people who find their ultimate fulfillment in only You. Sounds a little narcissistic to me."

This is typically our flesh talking, but in our honest moments, most of us have struggled to answer this inner critic to our satisfaction. C.S. Lewis wrote an incredible chapter called "A Word about Praising" in his book "Reflections on the Psalms." There, he ties how quickly we may praise an inanimate object like a picture or painting to praising God.

He says this:

> The sense in which the picture 'deserves' or 'demands' admiration is rather this: that admiration is the correct, adequate, or appropriate response to it, that, if paid, admiration will not be 'thrown away,' and that if we do not admire we shall be stupid, insensible, and great losers, we shall have missed something. In that way many objects both in Nature and in Art may be said to deserve, or merit, or demand, admiration. It was from this end, which will seem to some irreverent, that I found it best to approach

the idea that God 'demands' praise. He is that Object to admire which (or, if you like, to appreciate which) is simply to be awake, to have entered the real world; not to appreciate which is to have lost the greatest experience, and in the end to have lost all.
(Lewis, C. S. 1958)

When we experience something magnificent, it's a normal human reaction to tell others about it. We do so naturally and with great joy. If this is true of human relationships, how much more so with God? When we have found something of incredible worth, we are wired to lavish it with praise.

I love to give my wife great gifts. When I pick out a present, I want it to bring a smile to her face. I want it to be thoughtful and practical. I want her to feel as if I know her. God has a similar posture but with far more resources. He gave humanity great gifts. All of creation is available for our enjoyment, but He went one step further. He searched high and low for the ultimate gift capable of bringing us ultimate joy and eventually found it in a mirror. He created a people capable of containing His very presence. He made us in His image.

Instead of bemoaning God's nature, our hearts should praise His generosity. He wants to share Himself with us. Additionally...

BEGINNING WITH GOD'S HOLINESS GIVES US PROPER PERSPECTIVE

Praying first for God to be set apart is counter to our usual patterns of prayer. Even in the A.C.T.S model (Adoration, Confession, Thanksgiving and Supplication), we tend to rush through the "A" to get to the "S."

When approaching God, if we don't have established patterns of prayer, we tend to rush to the pressing circumstances we want dealt with immediately. Our felt needs then dictate our prayer lives.

This posture creates a variety of issues. We may end our prayer times feeling worse than when we started. When our minds are fixed on problems, they tend to multiply. This leads to emotional distress. Emotional distress then cycles back to mental anguish. After a while, we quit praying because we feel worse instead of better. Guilt and shame then begin to plague our prayer lives.

But how much different our lives can be when we start with God and His goodness in our lives, when we take time to remember His faithfulness and reaffirm our trust in His ability to handle our life circumstances.

Tim Keller puts it this way:

> When we put our needs/list first in prayer, we may grow even more anxious in and as a result of prayer, but when we start in worship, reminding ourselves how good and wise He is, when we get to our own needs, it is easier to put them in God's hands. Burdens come off rather than on me. (Keller, Timothy 2014)

PRAYER REORDERS OUR LOVES

Praying the Lord's Prayer reorders our desires. Apart from a proper view of God's power, love, justice and mercy, we will veer toward either pride or despair. We will become self-sufficient as opposed to God-dependent. We will then love good things more than we love God Himself. We will drift away from His design for our lives. We are wired to live in a relationship with God. Because He loves us, He won't answer prayers that fail to lead us toward finding our greatest satisfaction in Him. He wouldn't be kind if He did.

When we fail to praise Him, we miss out on something beautiful. When my kids were younger, we took a long road trip to the Pacific Northwest through Southern California and eventually back to Minnesota. Our kids were young. Miles on a map look different than miles in a car feel. Our children were disowned at least twice on our trip, and my wife and I were disqualified from the "Focus on the Family Parents of the Year" award due to our responses to the children.

One highlight of this trip was a visit to the Grand Canyon. I had been there before, but my wife and kids had not. I grew up a few hundred miles from the Rockies. They are an incredible mountain range. Coming from the east, the peaks gradually overtake the observer. What at first looks like a cloud is revealed as far more substantial. The closer one gets to the mountains, the more majestic they become.

The Grand Canyon is different. I've never felt the need to stay for days. I keep returning for the first few moments I see it. I walk on reddish rock, and then as if a door opens, I immediately see the canyon in all of its splendor.

It's incredible. If a canyon can take our breath away, how much more is the architect of the entire earth worthy of our praise?

There will be days God's beauty is gradual and comes slowly. In other moments it will arrive in an instant. In either case, we are instructed to honor His beauty above all others. We are to make His name holy above every other pursuit and desire.

We mustn't give up when we find ourselves dull in our spirit or unable to worship. When empty, praising God for His creation can be helpful, but another source may be even more beneficial. What was once viewed as hideous has grown to become something beautiful to me. When our hearts are distracted or disordered, look to the cross and the beauty it represents. Let Christ's work renew our minds and awaken our souls to the depths of His love.

This is to be our consistent discipline. It isn't easy. It happens over time, but it's worth the effort. If we are to grow in our prayer lives, we must learn to place God in the place of highest honor in our lives.

APPLICATION

THE FIRST STEPS OF SPIRITUAL DEPTH SHOULD COME FROM OUR WORSHIP, NOT OUR WORK

I'm a much better human doing than a human being. Give me a task, and I'll do it. Give me a plan for self-improvement, and I'll set to the task.

We like the measurable. We want benchmarks. Show us a standard so we can compare ourselves to others. Are we doing what we're supposed to be doing or not?

As we grow in faith, we realize our inner lives are broken apart from Christ. Even after coming to know Him, our flesh still tries to wield its control.

We work on inner development. We try harder. We might develop systems to ensure the dark parts of our inner lives remain inside. We might slap our wrists with rubber bands when we find ourselves gossiping, drop a quarter in a swear jar when we curse or place a few extra dollars in the offering before making a major purchase. We treat ourselves like Pavlov's dogs, trying to condition our inner being to catch up with the realities of the gospel.

Oh, what a wretched lot we are. But thanks be to God for all the work He has accomplished and done for us in Christ.

Spiritual depth doesn't occur when we work toward spiritual depth. Spiritual depth is connected to our worship. The more we see the extent of God's goodness, the more we elevate Him to the rightful place in our lives, the more we tend to grow. When the leaves of our spiritual branches stretch to the sky, our roots respond by increasing in depth. Making God our highest priority, affection and desire will, over time, allow us to grow as we are intended to grow.

Putting worship first is an excellent start in developing a healthy prayer life.

Additionally, I've found that keeping the Bible open to the Psalms is a great tool in sparking worship during my prayer times. They serve as a constant companion training my heart to worship. I've cycled through them several times in my prayer journey. Wrestling with the psalmists' varying emotions and circumstances allows me to relate their circumstances to my own or enter into the common struggles of humanity. A byproduct of the latter is empathy. In each case, I view the Psalm through the lens of Christ's work on the cross. Because of Jesus's suffering, circumstances once viewed as unfair now serve for my betterment and God's glory.

Haddon Robbinson sums up the heart of this chapter nicely.

> We often pray for God to increase our devotion and depth of spiritual life, but none of the petitions found in this prayer are for personal holiness. The first step in spiritual growth is not to pray for inner feeling or inner change but that God will indeed be God in our lives. The focus of the spiritual life is not experience; it is God. We have the command to be holy as He is holy because the spiritual life begins when we allow God to be God in all aspects of life—personal, family, business, recreation—and to let Him set us apart for His good purposes. (Haddon W. Robbinson 2016)

10.

YOUR KINGDOM COME, YOUR WILL BE DONE
PRAYING FOR GOD'S REIGN

I live in a nation where rulers change every two to six years. We alternate between which half of the country feels like they are being ruled by an evil dictator and the other slowly realizing their hopes for a utopian experience of either Democratic or Republican rule falls short of pre-election promises.

Different politicians have ruled over my life. Still, I have yet to experience the advancement of a foreign enemy seeking to bring a new type of governance over my existence. I'm grateful for my freedom, but as a result, I often fail to resonate with words like kingdom, reign and rule. The terms evoke images of royalty, knights in shining armor, crusades, and thrones from bygone eras or evil dictators or warlords at present.

When I try to superimpose these concepts onto their modern-day equivalents, praying for God's kingdom to come seems narrow. Is God asking us to specifically pray for His values to be advanced in our earthly political systems? Is He inviting us to pray for words written in His book to be copied and pasted onto sheets of paper in Washington, DC? Maybe, but it involves more than politics.

As a child, I assumed praying for Christ's kingdom meant we were to pray for heaven to come to earth. In my faith tradition, this involved a final world war, a possessed world leader, and the end of the planet as we know it.

Praying for an event inherently involving my early exit from this world before my honeymoon resulted in a lack of enthusiasm for this portion of the model prayer.

It was only much later, as I worked through the teachings of Jesus, that I began to realize the kingdom of heaven was not my eternal resting place. It was God's authority and influence over His creation.

God's influence is not relegated to physical boundaries like an earthly potentate who rules over a kingdom. When an ambassador represents a government in a negotiation, she speaks for her homeland's interests and brings the country's clout with her even while not on her native soil.

God's rule is powerful but yet to be fully realized. The war for the souls of humanity has been won, but battles still need to be fought. At present, many circumstances exist outside of His desires for humanity. Jesus walked the earth fixing situations outside of God's will. His frustration at people's stubbornness is evidence of His understanding of a world not as it should be. To encourage prayer for the will of God to be done, Jesus is hinting at a world not as it should be.

Through prayer, we are encouraged to join Him in His restoration efforts. We accomplish this when we transition from His goodness in worship (Hallowed be your name) to His purposes for our world. (Your kingdom come, Your will be done).

PRAYER FOR GOD'S KINGDOM ADVANCEMENT ALLOWS HEAVEN TO ENGAGE WITH EARTH

Why doesn't God snap His fingers and make evil disappear from our planet? Beyond the obvious loss of human life, He desires to work through humanity to bring about the fullness of His will. Sin, death, and the trials they create serve to purify His people and increase our faith.

In prayer, we withdraw from the resources of heaven to advance kingdom causes.

This should give us confidence in our asking. If we see anything outside God's will, we pray boldly, inviting His rule into our circumstances and lives. He may not answer our prayers as we expect, but we can trust in His ability to work all things for His glory and our benefit.

WE KNOW GOD'S WILL BY KNOWING AND PRAYING GOD'S WORD

Praying with the Bible open is a wonderful way to listen before we speak to God. It's also an essential guide in pointing us toward the will of God. As we read or even memorize His word, we slowly develop a proper perspective regarding His will. As we know it, we are instructed to begin praying for it.

This gives us confidence but should not be demanding. I've met people who prayed as if they could somehow bind God to His Word to get what they wanted. This is a teenage manipulation tactic. "But Mom, you always say...." It doesn't work on parents and doesn't work on God.

Praying through scripture allows us to pray specifically. Instead of vague appeals for God's blessing, mercy, or protection, it enables us to offer requests for specific needs. This helps us. As we wrestle through scripture, we learn to know our needs better.

Most of our praying for God's reign will be answered incrementally. To ask and keep on asking points toward the nature of kingdom rule. Our salvation is instant. God's rule is gradual. As a conquering king, He refused to crush any rebellion among His adopted children immediately. He instead empowers us to grow incrementally into who He saved us to be.

We must not give up. At times, even the content of our prayers needs to be shifted.

Andrew Murray, who has continued to shape the prayer lives of faithful Christ-followers long after his death, has this to say about our unanswered prayers:

> If no answer comes, we are not to sit down in the sloth that calls itself resignation, and suppose that it is not God's will to give an answer. No, there must be something in the prayer that is not as God would have it, childlike and believing; we must seek for grace to pray so that the answer may come. It is far easier for the flesh to submit without the answer than to yield itself to be searched and purified by the Spirit, until it has learned to pray the prayer of faith. (Murray, Andrew 1885)

We are more likely to press through unanswered prayers by rooting our requests in God's word. Instead of giving up, we can be confident that we are heading in the right direction.

PRAYING GOD'S WILL TRANSFORMS OUR FAITH

When we allow our fleshly requests to morph into mirroring God's will, our confidence will grow because we begin to ask for traits in line with what He wants in our lives and the lives of the people we interact with.

His primary goal is to work His heart and character within us for His glory. He will answer every prayer to this end. That said, we are still invited to ask for His involvement in every area of our lives. To fail to ask is to lose sight of God's faithfulness to provide for our needs.

We can pray for a spouse, a job and the necessary resources to make ends meet. We can ask God to use us to do great works for His kingdom. It doesn't mean He will answer each of these prayers as we would like Him to, but we are assured His answers will lead us to a place where we trust Him more. In this, even the "no" of God becomes a divine "yes."

A transformed faith is a persistent faith requiring flexibility. To avoid growing stubborn, we allow Him to alter our prayers, so He can do greater works than the ones we initially asked for.

Over time we will learn to confidently pray for God's will to be done but must also maintain a posture submissive to a plan we may not see.

PRAYING FOR HIS WILL TO BE DONE PROVIDES US AN OPPORTUNITY TO TRUST GOD WHEN OUR PRAYERS DON'T GOD EXACTLY AS WE EXPECT

Praying for God's will to be done isn't meant to take place with a sigh of resignation but instead should spark a healthy recalibration. When God's will occurs (even in opposition to our desires), we faithfully realign our lives in submission to His good work. We must regularly be shaken out of our complacency for this to happen.

Marriages tend to gravitate toward routine. Healthy marriages interrupt these patterns by adding elements of surprise and spontaneity. The occasional vacation, a night or two away from the kids, or a gift given on a non-obligatory holiday each help enhance a relationship. At times the unplanned events become the most memorable. Getting lost on a mountain hike leads to a shared moment watching a sunset or sparks a conversation needing to take place. Even our unexpected difficulties, arguments or relational tension can draw us closer to one another. A relationship forged and enhanced through overcoming life's obstacles or suffering is often richer and deeper than one characterized by prosperity and a life of ease.

The difference between marriage and our prayer lives is that God never gets lost, and nothing is wasted. When He disorients our lives, it is always for our benefit. I've had multiple ways I've envisioned my life unfolding. Many have yet to (or will never) take place. The trail to an eternal sunset is treacherous and filled with difficulty and pain, but putting one foot in front of the next will, over time, increase our faith in God's goodness and align our lives to reflect His priorities better. He has a plan to write a story far richer and more wonderful than I can write.

There is one last caveat.

WE CAN'T PRAY WITH GOD'S POWER WHEN WE FAIL TO SUBMIT TO HIS AUTHORITY

There is intrinsic submissiveness in the Lord's Prayer. To pray "Father," we must accept the terms of our adoption. To pray "Hallowed be your name," we agree that His name is worthy of being elevated above our own. To pray God's kingdom come and will be done, we submit our lives to His rule and plan.

It's difficult to ask God's kingdom to come into our finances when we cheat on our taxes. It's ineffective to pray for God to reign over a workplace while harboring bitterness toward a coworker for a past wrong. Praying for prosperity while withholding our money from God's control exposes an over-desire for the things of this world, and asking for a vibrant marriage while indulging in a pornography addiction is trying to pull a relationship in two opposing directions.

Let me be clear. Our perfection is not a prerequisite for prayer.

God wants us to bring our struggles and our difficulties to Him. We can confess our obstinance and even our pride. We are to live in the light even when what the light exposes isn't always pretty. God can always work with humility, honesty, and brokenness.

But as God shows us areas He wants to work on, we need to be obedient.

One of the greatest promises in the Bible is found in the first chapter of James. It is immediately followed by one of scripture's more confusing and misunderstood truths. The promise is connected to God granting wisdom through the trials of life. James says simply...

If you need wisdom, ask our generous God, and He will give it to you. He will not rebuke you for asking.

(It's the next part many have historically struggled with.)

But when you ask Him, be sure that your faith is in God alone. Do not waver, for a person with divided loyalty is as unsettled as a wave of the sea that is blown and tossed by the wind. Such people should not expect to receive anything from the Lord. Their loyalty is divided between God and the world, and they are unstable in everything they do. —James 1:6–8

When I viewed this passage through the lens of a major life decision, it felt crippling. I've never been 100 percent certain about any decision I've ever made. Even when signs and circumstances seemed to be lining up in an obvious direction, I still had doubts. This passage has brought me to tears as my lack of certainty made me feel like a wave of the sea tossed about by the wind.

This passage promises perspective, not a plan. Thus, instability occurs not when I fail to achieve 100 percent certainty regarding a decision, but when I fail to place my trust in God's perspective.

In context, James encourages his reader to ask for wisdom amid life's trials. The wisdom given is often connected to Christ-honoring actions and behaviors. He promises to clearly communicate how we are intended to obey and who we are supposed to be through our struggles. When this information is brought to light, and we instead choose to go in the opposite direction, we can't expect to continue receiving God's wisdom. We live with one foot planted firmly in this world and another tentatively placed in the next.

The advancement of God's kingdom doesn't necessarily include promises of healing every loved one in our lives, perfect children, or continual raises at work. He does promise to use His resources, every trial, and His Spirit inside of us to work toward building out within us the righteous character of Christ. God is always intentional through our trials. He will work everything for our good. This is a promise connected to our obedience. Our prayers will be hindered when we want the pleasure of our sin more than we want the blessing of God. If we remain hard-hearted, no technique, outline or creative idea will help our prayer lives.

APPLICATION

FIND A FEW TOOLS TO HELP IN PRAYING FOR GOD'S KINGDOM ADVANCEMENT

I'm looking forward to the day when I can talk to Jesus face to face. Any outline will either be unneeded or naturally flow from me in those moments. In the meantime, I need structure to help shape my times in prayer. I rely on God's Word to assist me in discerning His will and the nature of His kingdom. Listening to or singing worship music alongside reading and working through the Psalms may help elevate God to the rightful place in our lives.

When praying for God's will, I've encountered many faithful "list" people. A congregation member pulling out an old tattered notebook representing many petitions offered for the benefit of others is a great joy for a pastor. I'm humbled when my name makes it onto one of these pages, but I don't have one of these notebooks.

I've made attempts at praying through a list. When I move from one name to the next, I don't feel a sense of wrestling in prayer for the one I'm interceding for. I say their name, maybe with a few trite statements and move on to the next person in line. I never know when to remove a request. When I draw a line through a name, it feels like I'm shaking the dust off my feet or abandoning them to their fate. It is a good discipline, but I often leave my time feeling empty or ineffective.

With this being said, I still like the way people pray with their lists more than I like the way most of us don't pray at all.

God has wired us uniquely. Paul Miller goes into much greater detail in his book "The Praying Life" than I will here. He mentions using index cards as a great way to structure our prayers for other people.

I take an area I believe God wants to advance His kingdom and place it in the center of the card. Around the request, I add scripture and specific needs necessary to see the request answered or for kingdom fruit to ripen.

As a parent, I've struggled to pray with specificity for my kids. "God, I pray for my kids… Be with them…." Or, I'd excessively pray for their safety and protection. By taking time to write my requests on an index card, I find I'm more intentional about what I consistently ask.

I pray for my oldest to have complete knowledge of God's will and be filled with spiritual wisdom and understanding. I pray for his future spouse. I pray for favor in his relationships in school.

I may not pray everything on the card daily, but I have options and flexibility as I approach God's throne room with my request. I can add and subtract requests as they are answered or start over with a new card. If my kids, the church, our community, or the world have a new challenge or opportunity, I can easily add it to my prayer time.

It's not a perfect system. Sometimes I feel like I'm giving my dad a business presentation, but He knows the cards help focus my attention and allow me to be persistent and consistent in my prayers.

It's not the only way, but I've found it helpful in focusing my prayer times.

Our planet works according to the laws of sin and death, but through Christ, this power has been broken. Though Jesus refers to Satan as the ruler of this world, He also reminds us that He who is in us is greater than he who is in the world.

We have been given a mandate as the people of God to advance His kingdom through our prayers and obedience. Alongside our love for one another, these are the primary avenues He will bring about His power on earth. Our participation in this process matters. He delights in using us to bring about His will on earth. Pray for His kingdom to come and His will to be done.

11.

GIVE US THIS DAY OUR DAILY BREAD

PRAYING FOR GOD'S PROVISION

It seems simple. I can pray for bread.

When I pray, "Hallowed be your name," my disordered life comes into full view. Idols are revealed in my heart. I am exposed as spiritually dry, and with a busy day ahead, the equivalent of a therapy session with God as my counselor regarding my fleshly desires is daunting and seems self-centered. If I'm not careful, I find myself exalting my issues instead of exalting God's name.

Praying, "Thy kingdom come, and Thy will be done," forces me to know God's will. It requires reading His Word and knowing His heart enough to pray for it.

On the other hand, bread seems easy. It represents our basic human needs. I like praying for the resources I need to pay the bills and cover the cost of my necessities. Bread comprises the bulk of prayers offered to God. It seems simple, but it's not.

Our net worth (whether large or small) adds complexity to our prayer lives.

Some pray, "Father, give us this day our daily bread," with a pantry already full of food. Others have months of income in the bank in preparation for an emergency and are setting aside money for (or already have) a fully funded retirement account.

We pray, "Father, give us this day our daily bread" for items we already possess the resources to purchase. We might use the word "desperate" because it seems like a word we should use regarding our needs, but to some, the word rings hollow.

To be fair, part of the reason some live in prosperity is directly connected to their obedience to God's word. Faithfully giving, applying the truths found in the Proverbs and Jesus's teaching regarding saving for the future, and refusing to spend all they have on temporal pleasures tends to produce margin.

In addition, some are blessed to live in a country with tremendous affluence and opportunity. All of this may make pleading for daily bread feel disingenuous.

Others wish they were in this situation. For the stay-at-home mom, single parent, or one going through a season of unemployment, times when there is more month than money between paychecks may be the norm. With plenty or little, the struggle remains.

In these situations, we pray, "God, give us our daily bread, but if You don't, I have government assistance to ensure we're provided for." Or we could (and I'd even say we should) approach our church family regarding our financial needs. Most communities have food shelves available. Even those without disposable income typically (at least in most of America) can find what they need for their necessities.

When Jesus taught this prayer, He wasn't speaking exclusively to a poor audience; when it was recorded, He had all of us in mind. So how do we pray, "Lord, give us this day our daily bread," as God intended it to be prayed?

Before answering the question, it's important first to see the position of this request in relation to the other petitions in the Lord's Prayer. It comes after our worship and submission to His will. If we consistently begin our prayers with our requests and needs, we tend to make the handouts of God a greater priority than the hand of God.

Haddon Robinson reminds us of how dangerous this can be:

> When we pray, we often concentrate on the gifts in God's hand and ignore the hand of God Himself. We pray fervently for the new job or for the return of health. When we gain the prize, we are delighted. And then we have little more to do with God. If we are only after the gifts, God's hand serves only as a way to pay the rent, heal the sickness, or get through the crisis. After the need has been met, the hand itself means little to us.
>
> While God in His grace does give good gifts to His children, He offers us more than that; He offers us Himself. Those who are satisfied merely with the trinkets in the Father's hand miss the best reward of prayer—the reward of communicating and communing with the God of the universe. (Haddon W. Robbinson 2016)

Praying out of order also elevates our needs above the One capable of providing the resources necessary to meet them. In prayer, we will either see a big God or a big problem. A tiny object can easily obstruct the view of something more important behind it when we fixate on it. When our prayers are disordered, we may leave our times with the Lord more anxious than when we started.

When Jesus asks us to pray for our daily bread, He has more than loaves, scones and muffins in mind. A loving father will undoubtedly provide for our physical needs, but the bread from heaven extends further than yeast and dough.

Jesus once had a perplexing exchange between His disciples and Himself. He was ministering to a Samaritan community and hadn't taken a lunch break. His disciples were encouraging Him to pause for a moment and eat. He told them, "I have a kind of food you know nothing about." –John 4:32

This confused the disciples because accepting food from a Samaritan would have been frowned upon by most Jews.

He replied, "My nourishment comes from doing the will of God, who sent me, and from finishing His work." –John 4:34

Jesus was sustained spiritually by doing the will of God. When we pray for bread, we pray for the power to carry out God's kingdom plans. It's important to understand the connection between this petition and the last. The nature of God's kingdom advancement is impossible in the flesh or natural abilities. It can't be achieved solely through human initiative or resources.

There is a massive chasm between God's plan and our ability to carry it out. This desperation should create a healthy dependence upon God's power to carry out His purposes regardless of our economic status. The alternative to His provision is plastic fruit. The church is littered with dead trees adorned with what looks like kingdom fruitfulness. Living moral lives without God's power produces pride and self-righteousness. We become blind to God's work because we fixate on polishing our plastic so it appears genuine.

In general, I'm a loving and accepting person. I've taken pride in my ability to care for the people God has entrusted to me. I had an incident in ministry where I managed to argue, yell and grow increasingly frustrated with a congregation member – I remember driving home upset with the other person and myself. At this moment, a thought crossed my mind. "So, how's your love working out for you now?" The answer to this question became a turning point in my life. By exposing my inadequacy, I was prompted to exchange my ability to do anything good for God's ability to produce good through me. Instead of baking my own bread, I began to accept His provision.

THE SHADOW FOR THIS PROVISION ORIGINATES IN OLD TESTAMENT MANNA

The most important moment in human history was the life of Christ. Human history pivots on the incarnation, life, death, resurrection, and ascension of Christ. It represents humanity's only hope. Because of Christ's work, a bright and eternal future is before us. This event brings to light our future hope and produces rays of light shining throughout human history, creating shadows. The Old Testament, in particular, is filled with these images.

The Passover lamb was a shadow of Christ's sacrifice. The parting of the waters was a type of our deliverance through the waters of baptism. A shadow is not the substance but a faint outline of a reality yet to appear.

While the Israelites were wandering in the wilderness, they didn't have food to sustain them throughout their journey. They cried out to the Lord, who gave them manna from heaven. Each day they would leave their tents and collect enough for the day. The sweet, flaky substance was their daily bread and provision for their journey through the wilderness.

They weren't allowed to keep it overnight, or it would rot and be filled with maggots. God intended that they remain dependent upon Him for their provision each day.

Like us, they yearned for independence, resulting in a smelly tent needing to be aired out.

As we approach our Father in Heaven, we pray not simply for physical food for our bodies but for spiritual resources, including His Holy Spirit's work to move us toward the Promised Land. He doesn't provide for the entire week but is happy to give us all we need to get through the day.

We now live in the light instead of the shadows, but the same struggle for self-reliance exists in us when we pray.

WE MUST REMAIN DEPENDENT UPON GOD

Independence is never connected to spiritual maturity. Those who live as if it is will inevitably develop pride and false humility and drift away from community. Independence is one of life's great spiritual dangers. It brought the Fall in the garden. Why live under God's rule when we can call our own shots, live by our rules, and create our own future? We might still bargain with God in an "I'll scratch your back if you scratch mine" arrangement, but we maintain our autonomy.

Jesus modeled the opposite. "The words I speak are not my own, but my Father who lives in me does His work through me." John 14:10 He told the crowds, "I don't speak on my own authority. The Father who sent me has commanded me what to say and how to say it. And I know His commands lead to eternal life; so I say whatever the Father tells me to say." –John 12:49–50 Jesus modeled a maturity of dependence, not independence, down to the very words He spoke.

This dependence takes time and effort; for many of us, we find easier ways to get the will of God done on our own.

Paul Miller points out how this affects especially Americans.

> We (Americans) prize accomplishments, production. But prayer is nothing but talking to God. It feels useless, as if we are wasting time. Every bone in our body screams, 'Get to work!' When we aren't working, we are used to being entertained. One of the subtlest hindrances to prayer is probably the most pervasive. In the broader culture and in the churches, we prize intellect, competency, and wealth. Because we can do life without God, praying seems nice but unnecessary. Money can do what prayer does, and it's quicker and less time-consuming. Our trust in ourselves and in our talents makes us structurally independent of God. As a result, exhortations to pray don't stick. (Miller, Paul E. 2017)

Because we try to find alternative energy sources for living a spiritual life, we lack spiritual power.

We know what life is supposed to look like because we read our Bibles and go to church. Our souls yearn for the perfection of Christ but are unable to achieve it. This occurs partly because we don't ask God daily to ripen and cultivate what He has freely given us through His Son.

Dependence should be natural. I've not successfully produced one ounce of eternal worth apart from Christ. I can exercise faith and obey, but even these are gifts unavailable to me apart from the Holy Spirit's work in my life. This becomes even more apparent when I pray for God's kingdom to come in the lives of others.

I am responsible for my own will but am utterly incapable of controlling the will and desires of others. In my flesh, I use the tools of shame, guilt or human logic. Though these may alter outward behavior, they have little power to change the human heart.

As our hearts warm toward the needs of others, our desperation on their behalf in prayer becomes an opportunity for God to advance His kingdom through His love extended to them through us.

Ironically, a posture of desperation is a fertile ground for growth.

WE FIND HIS DAILY BREAD PROVIDES NOT ONLY FOR OUR SURVIVAL BUT ALLOWS US TO SPIRITUALLY THRIVE

If a billionaire told me he wanted to bless me substantially and then took me to the bakery and told me I could pick out whatever piece of bread I wanted, I would pick a flakey croissant with a honey butter glaze. But while I was eating the croissant, I would be thinking, "Thanks, but you said 'substantially bless,' and this feels a little weak."

When praying, "Father, give us this day our daily bread," we might mistakenly think God's goal is to provide the bare minimum for our lives. We falsely believe God is unconcerned about our wants and instead focuses solely on our necessities. Many Christians have been introduced to a God capable of much but is typically a little stingy with His blessings. This theology is often an overreaction to the teachings of the prosperity gospel. In one heresy, God exists to insulate our lives from suffering by blessing us with financial, circumstantial, and health-related prosperity. In the other, we begrudgingly endure poverty and suffering because we deserve nothing less. In Christ, even our suffering becomes part of the generosity of God. When experiencing financial prosperity, we can rejoice in the provision and the One who provided it. If we experience seasons of difficulty, economic hardship, or trial, we can celebrate God's promises to use even these to mature our faith and deepen our intimacy with Him.

We associate wealth with favorable circumstances and a healthy checking-account balance. God associates wealth with the wisdom, power, and love necessary to advance His kingdom despite our circumstances or net worth.

In Christ, the billionaire not only offered us a pastry but a company credit card with our name at the bottom. We simply need to requisition from Him daily the necessary power to bring about His will in our lives and those we interact with.

He's glad to do it. He loves us. Our asking does not put Him out.

APPLICATION

MAKE IT A HABIT TO ARTICULATE YOUR NEEDS TO GOD IN PRAYER

My journey in praying through the Lord's Prayer began as a teenager. I read a book meant to encourage praying through the model prayer as an outline. It included well-defined example outlines capable of helping me pray for hours. Its purpose was to help the reader find joy in prayer. Instead, its pages overwhelmed me, and I eventually gave up.

To pray every prayer in outline form is not the purpose of Jesus's instruction nor His example. The model prayer serves as a primary tool to help shape our communication with God in a way counterintuitive to human logic and fleshly desire. I've found it a great habit, but I don't follow an outline every day. There may even be days I don't spend an extended time in prayer.

The Israelites weren't supposed to keep manna for more than one night. There was one exception to this command. On the day before the Sabbath, they were to collect two days' worth of provision. Unlike weekday manna, this supply didn't spoil overnight. God's power is not relegated only to days we can maintain a lengthy quiet time. When our habit is to be full of His presence, missing one day will not hamper our effectiveness nor limit His provision.

This chapter aims to help the reader wrestle through

God's grace toward us and our dependence upon His daily provision. When we fail to form this habit, we are forced to feast on yesterday's manna. Entire ministries have devolved into serving maggoty leftovers. What was once alive and vibrant now carries the stench of human effort. Desperate dependence often builds a ministry. Independence and increased resources often contribute to it falling apart.

This makes a habit of articulating and asking for daily bread critically important. Opening the Bible to discern how God's kingdom advances will naturally expose a gap between what He wants to do and our ability to carry out His work. His provision fills this gap, and we are instructed to ask for it.

I've found it helpful to open up my calendar when praying for God's provision. I can bring up various appointments and possibilities I need His help in supplying my needs. My focus isn't always on success in what I'm trying to accomplish but on who I'm supposed to be through the process.

Lastly, there is a corporate nature to the Lord's Prayer. The outline is given with the entire church family in mind. I'm called not only to pray for my own needs but also the needs of others.

Jesus occasionally allowed His daily prayer routine to be broken to minister to the crowds, but His habit was to spend time with the Father. Ours should be as well.

12.

FORGIVE AND BE FORGIVEN

PRAYING IN LIGHT OF GOD'S FORGIVENESS

We all have relational scars.

I don't remember his name, but when I was four years old, an older bully pulled me aside on the preschool playground and twisted my arm behind my back at an angle, making me wonder if it was possible to dislodge my arm from my shoulder.

My brother once took a metal cap gun and clocked me between the eyes. In sixth grade, I had a classmate stab a pencil into my arm.

During my junior high years, I had multiple notes folded ever so delicately passed between classes to different girls at different times, asking if they would like to go out with me. I didn't know where we would go, but I made it simple. They had to check yes or no and hand it back to me the following hour. I remember most of those painful rejections. They hurt bad enough that I started including "maybe" or "I'll think about it" as additional boxes so they might let me down a little easier.

I remember multiple nicknames given to me during my high school years, branding me in the eyes of my peers. None were flattering or overly creative, but decades later remain memorable.

Growing up is hard, but it doesn't mark the end of our

wounds. Many offenses experienced as adults rival or surpass the difficulties of our childhood.

People either stuff any residual trauma deep within their souls, move on with a limp, or forgive.

In my speaking, I overstate to make a point. I work with people who have grown up in church settings with religious instruction. At times our numbness to spiritual truth might require me to overstate a principle to cause a healthy disequilibrium in their souls, sparking action or repentance. The following statement is not an overstatement: No one will mature in their prayer lives if they fail to forgive those who have sinned against them. If the road to heaven is a narrow winding path, unforgiveness is a tar pit trapping many from progressing in their walks with the Lord.

There are consequences when we fail to honor God's name in prayer. We miss His beauty. His love doesn't warm our hearts. Our minds fail to be renewed by the Gospel.

There are repercussions when we fail to pray for God's coming kingdom. We tend to grow self-absorbed. We live out lesser stories, forgetting the epic we have been invited to join. We grow stagnant in our faith.

There is a cost in failing to pray for our daily bread. We become like a few of the readers in the book of James. We have not because we ask not. We then lack the resources to carry out God's will in the world. We may grow wealthy financially but find ourselves spiritually anemic.

I can spell out these consequences logically and back up my deductions with various scriptures. When it comes to the forgiveness of sins, Jesus doesn't wait for or allow later apostles to inform His audience of the consequences of unforgiveness. Immediately following the Lord's Prayer,

Jesus says the following in the book of Matthew: "If you forgive those who sin against you, your heavenly Father will forgive you. But if you refuse to forgive others, your Father will not forgive your sins." –Matthew 6:14–15

With consequences so dire, one would think Jesus would begin His outline with the forgiveness of sins. He doesn't because the simple acknowledgment of our hurt fails to produce the desire to forgive. Only by understanding the depth of His love extended to us through Christ are we properly motivated to forgive others. This is (in part) why we begin praying by looking to God in worship.

Additionally, we are more apt to forgive others when we first address our faults.

WE PRAY 'FATHER, FORGIVE US OUR SINS' BEFORE WE PRAY TO RELEASE OTHERS OF THEIR SINS AGAINST US

Let's start with a good question: "Why do we need to be forgiven and confess sins already covered on the cross?"

Jesus paid for them all. Why do I need to rehash them daily? It seems like an exercise in negativity.

We can't, by our confession, atone for our sins. Jesus already paid for them.

In 1 John, the apostle reminds us that – "He is faithful and just to forgive our sins and to cleanse us from all unrighteousness." –1 John 1:9 This means that because of His sacrifice, it is not only allowable or permissible but right and just for Him to forgive us of our sins.

If our debt was canceled once and for all, why is it essential for us to continue confessing our sins? It's safe to say it is more for our benefit than His. Asking for forgiveness daily reminds us to walk in grace and humility. It serves as a recalibration in our lives.

Confession allows us to live in the light. God is always making adjustments in our lives. He molds clay, prunes branches, and refines metal. When we fail to grasp our propensity to sin, we walk precariously through this life in danger of slipping and falling. Many view sin as an event or an action. It can be. But most often, sin is missing the mark of God's best.

When I was younger, I often gauged my spiritual progress by the absence of specific actions in my life. If I could avoid alcohol, tobacco, premarital sexual activity, and the big swear words, I would be well on my way to sainthood. I remember being so confident in this model of righteousness that I picked up Chuck Swindoll's book "The Finishing Touches" in high school. It took me over one hundred pages to realize he was writing the devotional with more silver-haired saints in mind.

I still commit sins. Angry outbursts, a lack of patience, and judgmental thoughts still plague my life. I do wrong but also fail to do right. God's righteousness is not simply the absence of sinful behaviors but the manifestation of an obedient life.

While I carry around my crucified flesh, I will continue to sin. Until I love others as God loves them, I'm missing the mark of who He saved me to be. If not for the grace of Jesus, these truths would crush us. In Christ, the confession of sin gives us a proper perspective regarding our current spiritual condition.

When we ask God for forgiveness, we bring our shortcomings and deepest fleshly desires to Him. We bring Him our "I don't want to's," and "I'd rather not's." It's where we tell God, "I know you say I should do this, but I'd much rather do that."

We bring our weakness and cowardice, allowing the Gospel's power to transform us.

Let the following sink in: It is currently harder for us to be authentic and transparent regarding our spiritual condition than it is for Christ to forgive our sins. (Peter Haas 2022) The cross has already been accomplished. Every sin (past, present and future) was covered through this past act. In most instances, it takes longer for me to admit my sin than it does for Christ to forgive it.

When I focus first on the sins of others, I'm tempted to believe my issues are connected to their faults. I would be more loving, caring, and sympathetic if my coworker wasn't an idiot. I'd be far more patient if my spouse were more understanding. If my kids were better behaved, I would be a better dad.

God's encouragement in prayer is first to examine our own lives before we release others of their sins against us. We opt out of the blame game and allow God to see us as we are. Spiritual maturity is connected more to our eagerness to confess and our willingness to repent than a resume of flesh-produced moral behaviors.

These truths should motivate the following petition.

"As we forgive those who have sinned against us." –Matthew 6:12

In this statement, Jesus is not trying to cause trauma but to help mitigate its effects. There is a great deal of evil human beings can commit against one another. One might think I've gotten off lightly with a twisted arm and a few unflattering nicknames throughout my childhood.

Some have suffered repeated physical and sexual abuse. Others experienced workplace incidents setting off a chain reaction altering the entire course of a career. Half of marriages end in a divorce. The closer we allow ourselves to a person, the greater capacity we give them to wound us deeply.

By demanding forgiveness, Jesus is in no way minimizing sin. God certainly didn't. Our sin cost His Son His life.

Many churches teach the doctrine of all sins being equal. If we've committed one sin, we've committed them all. This statement is true regarding sin's ability to separate us from God's presence. Our righteousness is like a glass light bulb. When it falls to the ground and shatters, there is no way to put it back together. In this, a white lie and the acts of a serial killer produce the same results.

We are all sinners and spiritually dead. There is no ranking sin when it comes to those capable of preventing our entrance into heaven.

By these statements, Jesus never intended to communicate earthly sins' consequences as equal in magnitude. His death reminds us that He considers no sin trite. Each failure separates us from God, but some carry weightier consequences and cause more significant harm. In his letter to the Corinthians, Paul reminds his readers that sexual sins produce a more destructive result than other acts of disobedience because we sin against the temple of God or our bodies.

Regardless of the depth of hurt or the egregious nature of the sin, the command remains the same.

We must forgive others.

Before delving into the nature of what forgiveness entails, it may be important to explore what it is not.

1 – FORGIVENESS IS NOT SYNONYMOUS WITH FEELING REALLY, REALLY SORRY

I have met many people who are crushed by what they've done. They decided to open a bottle again or sneak out for one last date with a woman who was not their wife. They got caught, drunk, or incarcerated and came to me remarkably sorry. They were broken up about the repercussions of their choices, not the sin itself.

Sorrow is not the same as repentance. We can feel bad, but Godly sorrow is something entirely different. Sin is like a funnel. It appears wide and open but, over time, restricts and controls. Most people want the option to sin without the consequences of their actions. Anger over sin's effects differs from Godly repentance. In one, we desire to avoid the results of sin. In the other, we develop a distaste for the sin itself. We agree with God's truth about our transgression.

2– FORGIVENESS IS NOT FORGETTING

"Forgive and forget" is a terrible life motto. The first part is ok; the second is impractical and, at worst, harmful.

Some saints carry the weight of harboring unforgiveness even when they have released the one who sinned against them. They limp through life because their remembrance of an event serves as evidence of their failure to forgive.

There are certain offenses we will remember to the

grave. Forgiveness is not forgetting. It may even be unhealthy and unwise to forget an offense too quickly.

3– FORGIVENESS DOES NOT IMMEDIATELY RESTORE TRUST.

When we offer forgiveness, it means a lot, but it doesn't mean we act as if nothing has happened.

Upon getting mugged in an alley, forgiving our assailant is appropriate and good. This forgiveness does not mean continued trips to the same alley are wise. Jesus teaches turning the other cheek. This command is not an invitation to allow ourselves to be pummeled by an enemy. The strike in this text was most likely referring to an insulting slap, not a closed-fisted uppercut. To turn the other cheek did not encourage additional abuse but was instead the invitation to a continued friendship. The cheek was offered for a friend to kiss. It represented openness to the restoration of the relationship.

Forgiveness should be immediate, but a spiritually healthy person allows trust to be built back over time.

Let's transition to what forgiveness is.

FORGIVENESS IS SENDING THE SIN AND BITTERNESS AWAY FROM YOUR SOULS

Our souls are containers filled with living water. This water brings life and joy in the Spirit. The world does its best to poison the waters of our lives as we wound one another. Living water is living because it is always moving and replenishing our souls. When we fail to forgive, this water becomes stagnant. The vertical tube pumping in a fresh supply of God's grace becomes clogged. We can do our best to throw in chemicals of self-help techniques or otherworldly purifiers, but stagnant water is still stagnant. We may still remain moral, even basing our morality on a Judeo-Christian ethic, but the motives for our behavior will shift from pleasing God to appeasing God.

When Jesus spoke of how our refusal to forgive others results in the Father not forgiving our sins, the stubbornness in this statement rests in us, not Him. His commitment to forgive our sins included a cross.

We are saved through faith by grace alone, not our ability to forgive. However, habitual bitterness associated with unforgiveness may reveal that the truth of the Gospel has yet to sink into our souls. When we hold the sins of others against them, we fail to see the magnitude of God's forgiveness of our debts. Instead, we must dump out the bitter waters and allow living water to take its place.

FORGIVENESS IS GIVING UP OUR RIGHT TO GET EVEN

When I do premarital counseling, I have a session on conflict that most understand cognitively but fail to grasp completely. The couple tries, but learning to fight in marriage is a learned skill. In our time together, I bring up the use of trump cards. When laid in a fight, these cards represent a past offense capable of trumping any current transgression. They win arguments and are helpful tools capable of exacting vengeance for previous wrongdoings. When I lay a trump card, it makes my sin seem less egregious.

Some Christ-followers allow their previous hurts to

remain doused in gasoline. Their words say they have forgiven, and on most days, it looks as if they have, but a fresh new hurt creates a spark igniting a fire blazing over an entire relational history. Forgiveness gives up the right to use these past hurts to inflict new pain.

FORGIVENESS IS A REFUSAL TO TAKE WHAT ANOTHER PERSON OWES US

When first instituted, "an eye for an eye" was a radical concept because it ran counter to human instinct. A car ride with children under the age of ten will illustrate this dynamic. A finger extended beyond the accepted boundary of another sibling erupts into World War 3. What starts with a minor offense quickly escalates to verbal assault and eventually comes to blows. Human nature wants justice beyond what is taken. Break my finger, and I want your hand. Take an eye, and I want your head.

Jesus instead says to forgive. This doesn't abolish the justice system. It doesn't eliminate the consequence of every sin. It means I release the offender from the debt they owe me.

FORGIVENESS DOES NOT NEGATE WRESTLING

Superficial forgiveness is far more dangerous than wrestling with God through an offense. Complaining about one another should not be part of church life. Complaining to God is a part of healthy Christian growth. When we fail to release our offender completely, we may take an elevated position over the one who hurt us. Our quickness to pseudo-forgive another person may serve as Exhibit

A in our judgment of the one who offended us, alongside strengthening our case in a matter.

The Psalms are loaded with complaints about other people. David rails against enemies, former friends turned adversaries and even God Himself. The end of our wrestling must be forgiveness. We should consciously reexamine our sin, God's grace, and His heart toward the offender. When we do, we allow His perspective to begin to shape ours.

FORGIVENESS INVOLVES RESTING IN THE JUSTICE OF GOD

The most difficult people I've had to forgive in my life are Christians. To be fair, the closer the friendship, the deeper the potential for hurt. I also consistently dupe myself into believing those who know Christ are immune from wicked behavior. The church is not exempt from condescending speech, pride and, unfortunately, abuse.

I have stories of hurt where the perpetrator has likely failed to think of me for over a decade, yet their transgressions continue to mark my life. From my perspective, it appears they got away with their sin. There was no repentance, no reconciliation, or sorrow. They failed to grasp the depth of emotional pain they inflicted. The Spirit should have convicted them. I've yet to receive the phone call confirming their repentance. It isn't fair.

Part of my struggle has been rooted in a misunderstanding of the justice and judgment of God. I've often imagined heaven as the ultimate do-over. We arrive, our brains are washed of earthly memories, and we enter eternal bliss in a socialistic utopia where everyone is rewarded identically.

Jesus, while on earth, connected our sacrifice here to eternal reward there. Our identification with Him here results in honor there. Our financial giving here is returned exponentially there. Everyone stands before the holiness of God. Those who lack the substance of Christ will burn away like chaff. Those who know Christ will have their lives sifted and refined by the same fire. Part of what will be revealed during this moment is the substance and fruitfulness produced in our lives. Our works will be judged, and we will either harvest gain or suffer loss. Jesus placed His faith in this judgment.

In Peter's poem in the second chapter of His epistle, he says the following:

He never sinned,
nor ever deceived anyone.
He did not retaliate when He was insulted,
nor threaten revenge when He suffered.
He left His case in the hands of God,
who always judges fairly. –1 Peter 2:22–23

We don't need to retaliate when we live in light of God's justice. We don't have to threaten or carry out acts of subtle revenge. We instead trust God to judge fairly. This completely changes my outlook regarding those who sin against me. I figure either God will continue to shape and refine them in this life, or He will do the same on Judgment Day. In either case, only the best of who they are will remain. This truth helps me maintain a healthy fear of God and extend grace to others who are accountable for their actions.

Beth Moore reminds us of this truth.

God is not asking us to let 'it' go haphazardly into the black hole of nonexistence. Forgiveness means letting it go to God. Letting it go from our power to His. Forgiveness is the ongoing act by which we agree with God over the matter, practice the mercy He's extended to us, and surrender the situation, the repercussions, and the hurtful person to Him. (Moore, Beth; Crusade for World, Revival 2005)

APPLICATION

FORGIVE

I've withheld forgiveness for a variety of reasons. Most of which are rooted in pride. They don't deserve it. They weren't sorry enough. They failed to understand the depth of hurt they caused. When I've harbored unforgiveness, it only hurts me. It's been famously quoted: Unforgiveness is like drinking poison and expecting your enemy to die.

When I've grown bitter and unforgiving, I hurt others. Wounded people wound people. Ironically many people injure others in the same way they have been injured.

To pray to a God of grace, we must release others of the debts they owe us. When we fail in this arena, our worship dries up, our desire for God's coming kingdom is diminished, and the spiritual strength we need to grow is outside of our grasp. Forgiveness is necessary for our spiritual growth and vitality.

I want to end this chapter with one last encouragement.

SCARS CAN BREAK OPEN; IT DOESN'T MEAN WE'VE FAILED TO OFFER FORGIVENESS

I've had moments where seemingly out of nowhere, I find myself agitated or angry at someone I've already forgiven.

This created a sense of shame and guilt. I thought I forgave them. I began to wonder if my forgiveness was only partial or incomplete. Most wounds are scratches or nicks, barely breaking the skin. Over time they grow unnoticeable and are forgotten. Other wounds cut deeper. God's work of restoration in these instances involved more than a simple Band-Aid. He may have needed to field-dress the wound or reset a bone. Often these instances result in scars.

Scars remain visible. Every once in a while, the skin may become dry through difficult seasons and begin to crack. Blood may even seep through the skin. Remembering and resting in our forgiveness becomes an ointment and a bandage in such instances. This remembrance prevents the enemy from gaining a foothold in our lives. These experiences are not evidence of unforgiveness, but are often part of a spiritual attack on a vulnerable or tender area of our lives.

13.

LEAD US NOT INTO TEMPTATION BUT DELIVER US FROM EVIL
PRAYING FOR GOD'S DELIVERANCE

I invited my parents on a youth mission trip to St. Louis. It was an incredible week of ministry, shaping and stretching the youth and the volunteers. On one particular outing, we were tasked to take sack lunches and hand them out to the homeless.

The interactions were good. The youth had conversations and listened to stories of people often fading into the background of society.

All I remember from that day are a few good conversations and hanging out with the teens in my youth group. What my dad and mom saw that day was something they will never forget.

I grew up in a one-stoplight town. My dad grew up in a no-stoplight town. His graduating class numbered in the teens. City council members know not only their constituents on a first-name basis but also their pets. Diversity in this community meant there were farmers *and* ranchers.

He went to a Baptist church as a child and raised us in a similar church. The Spirit moved the same way every Sunday morning. There was a welcome, announcements, the first, second, and fourth verse of three hymns, an offering, the doxology, a sermon ending in an altar call during the final hymn, quickly shaking the pastor's hand, a few words of greeting afterward and then a race to the car to leave before one of the elderly ladies on their last driver's license backed out and hit us.

Within this upbringing, there wasn't an overemphasis on spiritual warfare. I'm sure it was brought up occasionally, but it was discussed more theoretically over coffee and doughnuts in a Sunday School class. With this as the background, my dad and mom took a group of teenagers and began passing out brown bag lunches in downtown St. Louis.

My dad, needing to model the courage necessary for the task, approached a lady and offered her a sandwich. She looked at him without saying a word and then stood on a park bench. I assume my dad thought it was odd, but as a good Midwesterner, wanted to start a conversation, so he introduced himself and asked her name. She responded with a name a normal parent would not name a child and spoke with a voice one would not expect to come from her body. Her eyes looked distant and vacated as she began to stretch her arms out wide and hover over my father, mumbling words he couldn't understand.

This was outside of my dad's wheelhouse. So, after a few moments, he looked at the woman and said, "I'll just put your sandwich here," and high-tailed it out of there.

The final petition of the Lord's Prayer reminds us of a spiritual battle being waged and fought outside of our physical realm.

Spiritual warfare is real.

A person's response to this statement varies widely

from church to church. Some seek mental health explanations and diagnoses to explain away any and all demonic oppression. Others cast out demons hovering over the Walmart parking lot, preventing them from a premium spot. When I try this, the Spirit prompts me to walk after reminding me of the maple long john I had earlier in the morning.

A proper posture regarding this battle is important. The Lord's Prayer ends with one final petition, "Lead us not into temptation, but deliver us from evil."

I've grown to appreciate this statement's placement in the model prayer. The prayer begins with God's greatness, transitions to God's plan, encourages us to ask for God's provision, reminds us of God's forgiveness and now ends with God's deliverance.

As for the final petition, the first phrase has brought confusion throughout the years, so much so that the Pope has reworded it in an effort to bring it in line with other teachings in scripture. We are first to pray; lead us not into temptation. Let me be clear.

THE ORIGIN OF TEMPTATION IS NOT FOUND IN GOD

Within every trial is a built-in temptation. In every difficulty we face, we must choose to either trust or distrust God. We will either do what He asks us to do or disobey. We will believe He is good or question His character.

God's purpose in a trial is to increase our faith and trust in Him. He will lead us into a trial but will not tempt us. We are not instructed to pray away our trials. To do so would be the equivalent of an athlete praying away the weight room, a student asking to be kept from school or a soldier praying to escape boot camp. Trials are intended to produce good within us.

Jesus, as our example, didn't fight the Spirit when led into an intense trial. Luke 4 describes His extended fast in the desert.

"Then Jesus, full of the Holy Spirit, returned from the Jordan River. He was led by the Spirit in the wilderness, where He was tempted by the devil for forty days." –Luke 4:1–2

The Spirit led Jesus into the wilderness. There He was tempted by the devil. God saw this moment as a necessary trial. The devil saw it as an opportunity to present options to Jesus, omitting the need for the cross.

Jesus was enticed by the opportunity yet did not sin. If Jesus was not immune from temptation, we must also be prepared.

Despite our new standing in Christ, temptations remain tempting.

Haddon Robbinson speaks to temptation's power.

> Temptation stirs the blood and inflames the imagination. If we were revolted by it, it would not be temptation at all. Occasionally we see where temptation will take us, and we may cry out for deliverance. Usually, though, temptation doesn't seem very bad, so we play with it and invite it into our lives. When we pray about our sins, it's not temptation that bothers us; it's the consequence of our disobedience that we want removed.

If temptation brought chains to bind us, we might resist it on our own. Instead, it brings flowers and perfume and promises good times and satisfaction. It bribes us with wealth and popularity and entices us with promises of prosperity and unbounded freedom. Only God can keep us from its charms. (Haddon W. Robbinson 2016)

The devil's playbook hasn't changed a great deal over the years. He continues to use the same techniques he's used since the garden.

HE WILL ENCOURAGE US TO OVER-DESIRE SOMETHING GOOD

Most days, we don't wake up wanting to go on a murderous rampage, steal a priceless work of art or light a Bible on fire. Idolatry is rarely the attraction to something evil. It is instead an increasing over-desire for something good.

Worshipping an idol throughout history was more than an allegiance to a carved piece of wood dipped in metal. It was an arrangement. If we give our worship, sacrifice, and allegiance, the representative god will bring prosperity to the home or village.

Prosperity isn't evil, but the over-desire for wealth is. Human sexuality is good within the bounds of God's intention but destructive when used to form our primary identity. Human relationships are meant for our enjoyment until we grow codependent upon others to define our worth. Being well-received is a good desire until we lie or fabricate a persona to find acceptance. Family is a blessing until it becomes the source of our identity.

The deceiver doesn't lead by asking for our submission. He begins by shifting our gaze from God to the blessings of God as our source of fulfillment.

HE WILL APPEAL TO OUR DESIRE FOR INDEPENDENCE

When our eyes shift from God's hand to God's handouts, we subtly grow more independent. We see what was created as good and imagine how we might use His creation to add glory or substance to our own lives. What was intended to be a blessing now defines us. Hard work, external beauty, intelligence, athleticism, or financial wealth shift from their original intention to become the central focus of our lives.

We then rearrange our behaviors to serve these lesser gods. The sacrifices they require are vast and extensive. They demand our financial resources, constant attention, and, regrettably, our families and close relationships.

They rob us of our peace, generosity, and love. We become self-centered instead of others-focused. What at first appears as independence quickly devolves into dependence. The pressure to maintain our value will begin to strangle us. The workaholic is forced to perform at a higher level than his coworkers or risk being defined as lazy. The beautiful woman is forced to have another surgery to maintain the illusion of lasting beauty. The intelligent man ceases to learn from others because he must be the most competent man in every room he enters.

What initially looks like freedom will grow to become slavery over time.

The devil would love for every knee to bow to him. He may eventually receive this type of allegiance from some. For the rest, he will settle for every other knee bowing down to anything other than God Himself.

HE WILL ENTICE OUR FEELINGS TO CHANGE OUR MINDS

Spiritual growth occurs when we believe and then rearrange our lives around God's truth. Transformation happens in our minds as we change the way we think. The devil will counter this pattern by appealing to our feelings and flesh. Jesus was hungry. This is a natural human experience after fasting for forty days. The devil used a God-given desire in an attempt to change Jesus's mind.

He did the same thing with Adam and Eve. He subtly encouraged them to question the goodness of God by appealing to their desires for the forbidden tree. "Did He really say...?" They succumbed to their longings instead of clinging to what they knew to be true of God. It's why Jesus responded with scripture when He was tempted. Instead of giving in to His desires, He focused His mind on what was true.

When we give in to temptation, and the result isn't as bad as we thought, we gradually change our minds regarding what is true. When we drift into lies and falsehood, we fail to shift reality. We may even distort the scriptures to justify our behaviors. Yet, God remains just, and the consequences for sin remain the same.

The devil's attacks on God's character aren't limited to the over-desires for the blessings of God.

Jesus calls Satan the ruler of this world. He didn't argue with the devil regarding his ability to grant sovereign rule over the nations. Beyond demonic control, he wields the power of sin and death. Every natural disaster, disease, accident, or oppressive regime are weeds produced by sin and death. God has chosen and may still choose to use any of these undesirable plants to bring about His judgment on wicked people. How and when He decides to do this is part of the playground mentioned in the chapter on the sovereignty of God. If and when this occurs, our response should be humility. Our Savior wept over the impending destruction of Jerusalem. Tragedy should produce our sympathy and grief, not create a little face time on a local or national news station where we spell out in great detail the judgment of God toward those facing severe trauma.

Through the resurrection, the power of sin and death has been destroyed. Neither can be used as a tool to separate us from the love of God. It doesn't mean their effects no longer hurt. A child with a cancer diagnosis, a fatal accident of a dear friend or a job loss can each create temptation. The wickedness of our enemy is great. He creates evil, then blames God for its consequences.

This makes the final petition of the Lord's Prayer vitally important. "Lead us not into temptation but deliver us from evil."

Let's examine what we're explicitly asking for.

TO BE LED

I'm a big fan of spiritual teleportation. I prefer to get from point A to point B by pushing a button. I am drawn to the idea of being filled with the perspective, wisdom, and faith produced by trials without actually needing to experience them.

In His divine wisdom, God has chosen to save us through trials instead of from them. This necessitates the guidance of God through more than a few hardships. The Lord's Prayer starts with God's fatherhood, and each request should be viewed with this relationship in mind. As a younger father, I remember my children as toddlers reaching up and grabbing one of my fingers. At times this happened when they were scared or in a crowd. We may have been moving from point A to point B, and they didn't want to get lost. I envision this prayer involving a similar sentiment.

The world is a scary place. It's easy to grow frightened when a routine visit to the doctor ends up with an unfavorable diagnosis, finances are tight, or our marriages fall apart.

I'm equally scared of navigating prosperity. The temptation to firmly root myself in a temporal world, trust in my wealth instead of trusting in God, mistake the blessings of God as an endorsement of sinful behavior or succumbing to the desire to hoard instead of give each make my next steps treacherous terrain.

Jesus's invitation is to look up, grab a finger, and allow ourselves to be led by a loving Father through every trial this life throws at us. Secondly…

TO SEE THE ONE WHO IS TRUTH AMIDST THE TWISTING OF GOD'S WORD

When Mohammad Ali boasted about his greatness, his confidence was admired by some and despised by others. Those who valued humility would have been repulsed by his declaration. Jesus's words were received similarly by the religious elite of His day. He had multiple "I am" statements, each layered with meaning and significance rooted in Israel's covenant with God, making Ali's claims seem small. On one occasion, He told His disciples, "I am the way, the truth, and the life. No one can come to the Father except through me." –John 14:6 In Christ, the truth became personified.

When confronting evil with truth, the church often makes one of two mistakes. The first is neglect. Many Christians live defeated lives because they are on the equivalent of the beaches of Normandy in an eternal fight much more important than World War II, wielding a butter knife as a weapon. They fail to spend time in God's Word or with God Himself.

The second group enters into battle knowing God's Word yet fails to understand God's heart. Spiritual warfare is then fought in equations. This scripture plus this truth multiplied by this passage must always equal this result. This method removes nuance and fails to consider the complexity of God's kingdom advancing in a sinful world.

When we see Jesus as the way and the truth, we are encouraged to look at His example, discern His heart toward others and respond accordingly. When tempted to distrust God through a trial, we find a definitive truth connected to the cross. God's love for us has been settled.

We can cling to this certainty during extreme difficulty. Our suffering is now a privilege in its testimony and what it produces in us.

When Jesus was tempted, He could withstand the enemy's onslaught because He knew God's Word and the heart of God Himself. God's Word is not only true; it needs to be true in us. Prayer rooted in the scriptures helps prepare us for any attack the enemy may levy against us.

APPLICATION

DISCIPLESHIP, NOT DELIVERANCE, IS THE KEY TO VICTORY IN SPIRITUAL WARFARE

Or maybe discipleship is the path to deliverance.

The disciples, during their time with Jesus, ran into a problem. Their teacher had given them the authority to cast out demons and perform miracles in His name. It was great. They were wielding the power of heaven on earth. They performed miracles and cast out demons. As they moved from village to village, they grew in popularity and potentially pride. Toward the end of this season of ministry, they were confronted with a small child possessed by a demon. They tried all of their typical methods and tricks, but each of the twelve failed to cast it out. My guess is they had accomplished much more on their journey than healing a small boy, but their failure forced the child's father to bring the little one to Jesus. The demon was a nasty spirit causing the boy to foam at the mouth, gnash his teeth and would occasionally make the child throw himself into a fire in an attempt to end the boy's life.

Jesus cast the demon out, but later the disciples

approached their teacher privately and said, "Why could we not cast it out?" –Mark 9:28 Jesus responded that this kind only comes out through prayer and fasting.

I don't think Jesus intended the disciples or us to spend much time categorizing demons into the ordinary run-of-the-mill demon versus the far superior "fasting and praying" demon.

Instead, we should pay attention to the spiritual disciplines Jesus listed as the key to victory. The disciples had drifted from the source of their power and began to wield their own. Before we seek deliverance, we first need to spend time with the Deliverer. Others in the book of Acts sought to use Jesus's name as an incantation without living under His authority, and they walked away from the incident naked, bloody and beaten.

Our lives will fail to experience the blessings of Christ until we move from declaration to discipleship. We cannot simply claim to believe in Christ; we must also follow Him.

To grow, we need to engage in the spiritual disciplines. We must pray, fast, read scripture expectantly, develop a heart of generosity, and spend time meeting with God's people.

Those who cultivate these disciplines consistently have a far greater chance of finding spiritual victory in this life than those who attend the class Exorcism 101.

LET THE GOSPEL RENEW OUR MINDS

When I pray through the petitions of the Lord's Prayer, I've found it helpful during this final request to remind myself of the truth of the Gospel. As a good evangelical Christian, I have been taught the importance of the Gospel for salvation, but often lost is the Gospel's power for our sanctification.

Jesus came to earth as our great example, born as a sinless man. I will walk in His love and under His authority.

He died on the cross for the forgiveness of our sins. I will move through my day in grace.

He rose again from the grave. The power of sin and death has been destroyed. My flesh is now crucified. It still flops around on a cross, causing me grief in this life, but it will eventually be destroyed. If today is the day I die, death (once final) is but a shadow of its former self. Nothing can separate me from Christ's love.

He is now ascended to a place of authority and power. My circumstances cannot draw me away from Christ. By faith, I will treat my trials as a gift drawing me closer to Him.

He has given us His Holy Spirit. Jesus sent the deposit of His Spirit as a promise of an even greater future return. The Holy Spirit's primary work is to provide the power necessary to live a Godly life. The Spirit unifies and equips the people of God to do great works.

I've found that renewing my mind daily around these kingdom truths helps give me both the perspective and power necessary to fight temptation.

14.
OUR
A FINAL WORD ON PRAYING TOGETHER

The priesthood of all believers does not mean simply or even first of all that each of us is our own priest, but it means, above all, that we are all priests for everyone else. (González, Justo L. 2020)

My parents were faithful in their church attendance.

If the doors were open, my sister, brother, and I would be there.

We went to church Sunday morning, Sunday evening, and Wednesday night for either my third sermon, a prayer meeting or a monthly business meeting.

I was in church a lot. I learned to doodle and draw on the bulletin, and as a result, I have excellent penmanship. I would work on my cursive while the pastor worked through the minor prophets.

The business meetings were the toughest. I was smart enough not to take accounting and advanced economics in high school. But as a child, I was forced to park myself on a hard wooden pew and listen to someone report monthly on church math.

Unfortunately, the prayer meetings were only slightly better than the business meetings. I would try to listen as a dear woman would go over the findings of her latest doctor's visit alongside a recap of anyone she ran into in the waiting room. We would then pause and pray over a potential knee replacement, heart condition or nagging toe fungus.

Another saint would then stand and take ten minutes to describe an accident their son's friend's relative's dog's former owner had three states away.

Eventually, we would work through our unspoken prayer requests. The pastor, over time, learned that if there was one unspoken request, there were probably more, so instead of praying for each hidden hurt, he asked for a show of hands, and we would efficiently pray for the entire batch as a whole.

The pastor might periodically ask about any praises or thanksgiving we might like to share. This was code for people to talk about the achievements of their grandkids or kids for a few minutes.

By the time we ended the evening, there was often more storytelling and information dispensing than prayer.

I'm not proposing we cease praying for these types of requests. We should maintain an ongoing dialogue with Jesus regarding major purchases, health issues, and tragedy, even if it doesn't directly affect us.

I also want to be clear; I love the church I grew up in, and I appreciate their attempts at corporate prayer. Their attempt was better than many churches' lack of trying.

I understand the difficulty more now than I did in my youth. Private prayer is awkward. Corporate prayer, for most, means the same awkwardness in front of other people. Most of us respond to this public discomfort by learning the importance of crafting our public prayers ahead of time so we don't sound like an idiot. We learn the necessity of knowing how to end our requests so we don't ramble on without a clear path to land the plane. This helps our prayers avoid the need to mumble an indiscernible closing remark before a definitive amen.

This dynamic creates tension as we drift from having a direct conversation with God to being hyperaware of others in the room.

Prayer is difficult in group settings but is also essential to a growing faith community. There is an overarching theme within the model prayer tied to the corporate church body.

"**Our** Father who art in heaven. Give **us** this day our daily bread. Forgive **us** our sins as **we** forgive those who have sinned against **us**. Lead **us** not into temptation. Deliver **us** from evil." –Matthew 6:9– 13 (emphasis mine)

Jesus didn't teach His disciples to pray, "*My* father who art in heaven. Give *me* my daily bread." The prayer is set up to encourage us to pray with the entire body in mind.

WE ARE CALLED TO PRAY FOR OTHERS INDIVIDUALLY

Andrew Murray presents an accurate word picture when he suggests…

"Private prayer is the root where corporate prayer is the tree. For the corporate tree to stand, the unseen roots must be strong individually."(Murray, Andrew 1885)

The Bible describes God's people as one body with many parts, a temple with many bricks and a singular bride made up of many people. To pray as God asks us to pray, we must shed our Western individualism and remember our interconnectedness with one another.

We are not lonely pilgrims on a journey to the Promised

Land. We are a mixed bag of people stumbling forward with different struggles and varying degrees of spiritual maturity. We are to be priests on behalf of one another.

Jesus instructs us to intercede with others in mind. We learn to pray individually in order to better pray for those who are weak, hurting or in a season of testing.

When viewing the Lord's instructions through a corporate lens, it changes the way I pray. I can elevate God's name to its rightful place when I see God work in my life as well as the lives of others. I pray for His coming kingdom in my own experience, but even more so in my faith community. I ask for my own provision but also remain aware of the needs of others. I'm incapable of asking for forgiveness on behalf of another individual, but I can still pray for the removal of roots of bitterness in my church. There are also certain sins entire groups commit. When confessing his sin, Daniel treated his nation's sins as his own. Many churches can corporately ask God to forgive them for their drift into Christian nationalism, a failure to be concerned for the poor, a disregard for human life, idolatry, materialism, prayerlessness, or a lack of evangelism. To avoid temptation, we can pray for the Gospel to become central to our daily lives, but it must also remain central in our corporate teaching.

When the roots of individual prayer fail to grow deep, the tree trunk will have difficulty staying upright, and the leaves will begin to wilt. Corporate prayer will lose its effectiveness and devolve into a performance.

CORPORATE PRAYER HAS THE POTENTIAL TO UNLEASH THE POWER OF GOD INTO OUR CHURCH AND COMMUNITY

When the church fails to pray, we build walls instead of attacking gates. The prayerless church fortifies its position in the world with an eye toward protecting those inside its walls from harmful outside influences. As this occurs, evangelism becomes less relational and devolves into throwing truth bombs over the wall of our comfortable structures. We yell from our secure tower... "Abortion is wrong!," "Marriage is between one man and one woman!" or even "Jesus is the way, the truth and the life." Our messaging alters depending on our structure's political bents. We become satisfied with our corporate alignment with the truth without regard to how the truth might be received. When the church fails to pray, these bombs explode onto social media or ink on an editorial page without God's power behind His truth. We fight God's fight without loving God's enemies. We repeat God's words without the breath of God's Spirit.

The gates of hell will not prevail against the advancement of God's kingdom. Gates are terrible offensive weapons. I suppose one could do minor damage if they were made of iron and pointy. Gates aren't intended to gain ground. They are designed to protect ground. God promised the disciples that the world would be turned upside down through their confession of Jesus as the Messiah.

God's kingdom advances best when His people learn to pray. Every great evangelistic movement in history was connected to the faithful prayer of the saints.

Tim Keller reminds us what this might look like:

Spiritual revival or renewal is a work of God in which the church is beautified and empowered because the normal operations of the Holy Spirit are intensified. The normal operation of the Spirit includes: conviction of sin, enjoyment and assurance of grace, the Father's love, access to the presence of God and creation of deep community and loving relationships. (Keller, Timothy 2005)

These characteristics differ from the content conveyed in most church prayer lists. It's been famously said that the church (when she prays) often spends more time praying sick people out of heaven than lost people out of hell. The root of much of this tendency rests in our lack of vulnerability. Our unspoken requests, in most cases, should be spoken. We often want prayer for our physical healing instead of confessing our waning belief in the goodness of God amidst our suffering. We pray for a change in circumstance when God desires to increase our faith and change our hearts. The power of God is advanced best in our weakness. When we conceal our frailty, we live in darkness and lack the fellowship promised when we live in the light.

APPLICATION
PRAY

There are many incredible books on prayer. Some help the reader pray specifically for their families; others are testimonies of God's amazing work through persistent prayer. Anemic ministries comprised of only a handful of people explode into reaching thousands because of their congregation's commitment to making prayer a primary focus.

I'm not a pastor of thousands of people. I preach in a church with pews, a steeple, and a sign with the potential to display clever sayings (often capable of doing more harm than good). I'm a proficient public speaker with a theater background who, several years ago, decided my natural talent was a poor substitute for the Spirit's power. I began to rearrange my day around praying through the Lord's Prayer. It's been a journey. I wrestled in worship until I started engaging the Psalms to help enhance my praise and expand my dialogue. I struggled in praying for others before allowing the Gospels and the Epistles to shape my petitions for those I serve. I still struggle with confession, which leads to pride.

As an author and speaker, I'm willing to wrestle through the scriptures and complex topics. I have a penchant for word pictures, a few of which lose their value when pressed too far (I nearly failed my ordination interview when I equated systematic theology with dissecting the family dog).

Let me bring this book to a conclusion with one final word picture. In His famous parable, Jesus described the Gospel seed being cast out and landing on different soils. I don't believe He was describing what was destined to happen, but what had happened up to that point in His ministry. The same good news was preached, but the people's reactions varied from disinterest to complete acceptance. At times the ground was hard. Other times it was weedy. In some cases, it was fertile.

My prayer is for this book to remove rocks and weeds

from the souls of those who read its pages so the kingdom of God can take root through our prayers. I failed to fully answer every question proposed in the first section of this manuscript, but answering the unanswerable was never my intention. Our wrestling tills the soil, preparing our souls to receive His truth. The Lord's Prayer then serves as a trellis. It provides a structure necessary for the plant to flourish. As we remain in Him and He in us, we will bear much fruit. My prayer for those who read these pages is to produce eternal substance as a result of their times in prayer, but even more important, I want those I serve through this endeavor to more intimately know Jesus Christ.

BIBLIOGRAPHY

Batterson, Mark. *The Circle Maker: Praying Circles around Your Biggest Dreams and Greatest Fears.* Grand Rapids, Mich: Zondervan, 2011. http://whelprimo.hosted. exlibrisgroup.com/openurl/44WHELF_NLW/ 44WHELF_NLW_services_page?u.ignore_date_ coverage=true&rft.mms_id=99970529102419 https://tcdlibrary.ldls.org.uk/vdc_100059600594.0x 000001.

Cymbala, Jim. *Fresh Wind, Fresh Fire.* United States: Zondervan,, 2001. sound recording, 6 sound discs : digital ; 4 3/4 in., 0-310-23649-5 Zondervan.

González, Justo L. *Teach Us to Pray : The Lord's Prayer in the Early Church and Today.* Grand Rapids, Michigan: William B. Eerdmans Publishing Company, 2020.

Haas, Peter. "Maturity Defined." In *Intimacy.* Substance Church, 2022. Sermon.

"Kingdom-Centered Prayer." Redeemer City to City, 2005.

Keller, Timothy. Prayer : Experiencing Awe and Intimacy with God. New York: Dutton, Penguin Group USA, 2014.

Lewis, C. S. *Reflections on the Psalms.* 1st American ed. New York,: Harcourt, 1958.

Miller, Paul E. A Praying Life : Connecting with God in a Distracting World. Colorado Springs, CO: NavPress, 2017.

Moore, Beth, and Revival Crusade for World. Praying God's Word : Breaking Free from Spiritual Strongholds. Farnham: CWA, 2005.

Murray, Andrew. With Christ in the School of Prayer. London: Nisbet & Co, 1885.

Nee, Watchman. *The Prayer Ministry of the Church.* Anaheim CA: Living Stream Ministry, 1995.

Packer, James I., and Carolyn Nystrom. Praying: Finding Our Way from Duty to Delight. Leicester: Inter-Varsity P, 2006.

Peterson, Eugene H. *Answering God : The Psalms as Tools for Prayer.* 1st HarperCollins pbk. ed. San Francisco: HarperSanFrancisco, 1991. Publisher description http://www.loc.gov/catdir/description/hc044/90055836.html.

Robbinson, Haddon W. *Jesus's Blueprint for Prayer.* Discovery Series. Grand Rapids, MI: Our Daily Bread Ministries/ Discovery House, 2016.

Whitney, Donald S. *Praying the Bible.* Wheaton, Illinois: Crossway, 2015.

Yancey, Philip. *Prayer : Does It Make Any Difference?* Grand Rapids, Mich.: Zondervan, 2006. Table of contents only http://www.loc.gov/catdir/toc/ecip0610/2006009434.html

Publisher description http://www.loc.gov/catdir/enhancements/fy0633/2006009434-d.html.

TEACH US TO PRAY

PRACTICAL WRESTLING AND A CHRIST-GIVEN MODEL TO ENHANCE OUR PRAYER LIVES

Travis Blake

Support Teach Us To Pray by rating and leaving a review on Amazon and sharing your experiences on all social media platforms.

Follow Travis Blake on Twitter, Facebook and Instagram

@travisblake76 on Twitter
pastor_travis_blake on Instagram

Printed in the United States
by Baker & Taylor Publisher Services